EVERYMAN,
I WILL GO WITH THEE
AND BE THY GUIDE,
IN THY MOST NEED
TO GO BY THY SIDE

EVERYMAN'S LIBRARY
POCKET POETS

JAZZ POEMS

••••••••••••••••••

SELECTED AND EDITED
BY KEVIN YOUNG

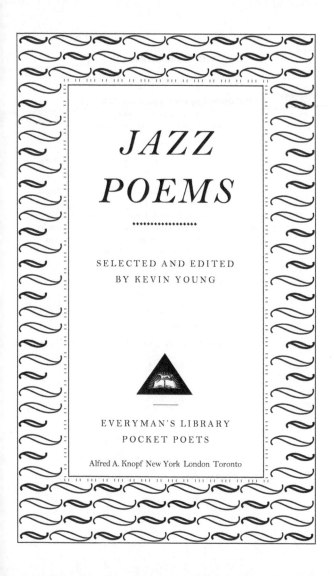

EVERYMAN'S LIBRARY
POCKET POETS

Alfred A. Knopf New York London Toronto

THIS IS A BORZOI BOOK

PUBLISHED BY ALFRED A. KNOPF

This selection by Kevin Young first published in
Everyman's Library, 2006
Copyright © 2006 by Everyman's Library

Fifteenth printing (US)

A list of acknowledgments to copyright owners appears at the back
of this volume.

All rights reserved. Published in the United States by Alfred A. Knopf,
a division of Penguin Random House LLC, New York, and in Canada by
Penguin Random House Canada Limited, Toronto. Distributed by Penguin
Random House LLC, New York. Published in the United Kingdom by
Everyman's Library, 50 Albemarle Street, London W1S 4BD and
distributed by Penguin Random House UK,
20 Vauxhall Bridge Road, London SW1V 2SA.

www.randomhouse.com/everymans
www.everymanslibrary.co.uk

ISBN 978-1-4000-4251-7 (US)
978-1-84159-754-6 (UK)

A CIP catalogue record for this book is available from the British Library

Typography by Peter B. Willberg

Typeset in the UK by AccComputing, North Barrow, Somerset

Printed and bound in Germany by GGP Media GmbH, Pössneck

CONTENTS

FOREWORD

Chocolate, cranberries, jalapeños, turkey, alligators, avo-cadoes (or *alligator pears,* as they were once known), *tobacco, corn*: all are native to the Americas. It can be a useful exercise to remember what first emerged here in the New World, or the western hemisphere, or the Americas—or however you choose to name this place of violent discovery and re-creation. One of my first teachers even wrote a book based on recipes using only food from this hemisphere; you haven't lived till you've tried avocado-cranberry ice cream with chocolate sauce. And like that ice cream, sometimes the unlikeliest com-binations, made possible by this place, manage to work.

To this list of American originals we may add jazz. First created by the descendants of African slaves, born of the blues in New Orleans, raised in Chicago and along the Mississippi, jazz has since visited hot Chicago and the cool West Coast, got run out of New York, spent April in Paris and a Night in Tunisia, and has even traveled to outer and inner space. Chocolate sauce indeed! It is a journeyman's music, not just because it was first performed in Storyville sporting houses, or in nightclubs, but because the music itself undertakes a journey, moving us on the dancefloor or in our chairs or even at a New Orleans-style funeral.

The origins of jazz are somewhat clearer than the

origins of the term "jazz": some say it's an African word; others say it's a shortened form of the jasmine added to perfume to "jas" it up; still more say it's short for Jasbo or the abbreviation for James, an early, mythic musician; others detect a more sexual meaning. What's more, some of the music's best players and innovators hated its very name. We could call it American classical music and be done with it.

Or, we could remember what the great Louis Armstrong said when asked to define jazz: "If you have to ask, you'll never know."

Still, this anthology, if it can't define jazz, does celebrate it through some of the best poems written about the music that changed our world, and even our words. *Swing, dig, vamping, hot, cool* and *free* will never be the same since jazz came along. Like my earlier anthology, *Blues Poems*, to which this collection forms a natural companion, *Jazz Poems* starts with Langston Hughes. Hughes was not the first to write about jazz—Carl Sandburg was technically a few years earlier—but Hughes was arguably the first to fully embody a jazz aesthetic, going beyond either the label or trend of jazz to have it affect his poetic language. Poems like his "Jazzonia" attempt to re-create the feeling of hearing jazz, the jazz experience; "Jazz Band in a Parisian Cabaret" or "The Cat and the Saxophone (2 a.m.)" go further, capturing the language of jazz, its very grammar. In these poems, most from the 1920s, Hughes seems to be playing the changes and even inventing a few of his own that we are still catching up with today.

The rest of this book's first section can be thought of as that other jazz tradition, trading fours, as each poem provides a sort of solo answered or ignored by the next. This is not to say that jazz, even early on, is without controversy—rather, Vachel Lindsay's "The Jazz of This Hotel" stands in for a number of poems (and many more editorials) questioning the music's seeming atonality, disharmony, amorality, and downright noise—opinions that crop up perennially. But jazz can take it. The result is a lively opening set of jazz poems, mostly from before World War II; though Gwendolyn Brooks' poem was written a few years afterwards, I couldn't think of a more fitting end to our introduction to the jazz poem.

Just as Louis Armstrong is said not only to have revolutionized singing—making his voice an instrument—but also to have made the jazz solo and his trumpet tell a story, the rest of this anthology follows a kind of rough history of jazz itself. The second section starts in New Orleans with the unrecorded (by wax, not by legend) early genius Buddy Bolden, followed by innovators Jelly Roll Morton and Louis Armstrong (known as "Pops" or "Satchmo," depending whom you ask). We then move north and east to consider elegant Ellington and his cutting-edge band.

However, readers looking for an exact jazz history won't find it anywhere, much less here—instead, history has helped group what are essentially a range of poems responding to, imitating, or chronicling a music as varied as the poems themselves. Certainly not all great, or even minor jazz artists have a poem worthy of them; what's more, poets often seem to center on major figures again and again. Charlie Parker, John Coltrane, Miles Davis, Charles Mingus, Billie Holiday: all have any number of poems about them, and indeed, in the case of someone like Coltrane, can even be said to have created a kind of poetics. (Sascha Feinstein, whose fine books on jazz poetry, and his two *Jazz Poetry Anthologies* with Yusef Komunyakaa, are crucial to the field, dubs this the "Coltrane poem.") In the pages that follow, several of these figures command sections loosely based around them, or their innovations— whether it's the bebop Charlie Parker helped invent, or the "sheets of sound" that Coltrane summoned.

As you'll see, poems about jazz seem especially willing to experiment, encouraged by the music to take chances. It's interesting to see how early such experiments happen. The form of jazz, even when seemingly formless, has spurred poets on to play with language and line in order to evoke that jazz feeling of risk. If, as

I said in my foreword to *Blues Poems*, with the blues the form fights the feeling, with jazz *the form is the feeling*. Perfected yet unpredictable movement; the ability to tell a story without words (as in Armstrong); the ability to contain blues feeling (returned to by Charlie Parker); pushing form to express the inexpressible (Coltrane); treating the instrument as a voice (Miles Davis), and the voice like an instrument (Billie Holiday): in its variety and vision, in its shifting choruses, jazz contains multitudes.

While jazz has, from its very beginning, inspired experiment, in poetry it has just as often inspired elegy. Indeed, poems on Bird and Billie Holiday and Coltrane often insist on both—a testament, I think, not just to the jazz lifestyle but also to the blues feeling at the heart of jazz, its quality of memory. This book's portable size prevents us from properly showing them all—much less capturing the elegiac feeling the country shared in the wake of Hurricane Katrina and its devastation of the Gulf Coast. All our nation, and its most native music, mourn New Orleans now. Still, even at its most elegiac, jazz attempts to make do, and make meaning of life in all its forms. "Life is jazz-shaped," Ralph Ellison once wrote, and the poets here seem to agree, and shape their poems accordingly. I have recently also come to think that the opposite is true— jazz is life-shaped—a distinction that recognizes not only the importance of jazz, but also that jazz, as much as any other music, may measure our lives best.

"Jazz is the art of discovery," writes David Lehman in a poem from *The Daily Mirror*, one of several books that emerged from his commitment to writing a poem a day for an entire year. Such an attempt, its necessarily improvisational quality, comes from jazz and from the New York School poets such as Frank O'Hara and painters such as Jackson Pollock, inspired earlier by jazz's insistence on the moment. Such experiments, like those of the Black Arts poets responding to Coltrane's death (as Haki Madhubuti and Amiri Baraka do, even riffing off each other) and to free jazz (calling it the New Thing), seem to me more lasting than those that sought in jazz neither freedom, nor form—both of which are inseparable, jazz seems to say—but rather a kind of fast-talkin' formlessness. Jive.

You won't find any easy "bop prosody" here, among the fine surrealist lines of beat poet Bob Kaufman, or in the improvisatory experiments of Harryette Mullen and earlier Kenneth Rexroth, or in the word and sound experiments "in sound variegated lit" by N. H. Pritchard. Still, many of these poems were actually written for, or even composed while, being read. Further, poets like Yusef Komunyakaa and William Matthews often write about the figures of jazz, telling both their own and their subject's history—which is to say, like jazz

16

itself, turning personal expression into public property. "Soul and race are private dominions," writes Michael S. Harper, another of the finest poets here, and both body and soul, midnight and heartache, are discussed by poets of all tenors.

"The rhythm of life is a jazz rhythm, honey. The gods are laughing at us." Hughes' line also knows that, like the blues, such laughter may be laughing to keep from crying—and there's a blues tone in even the most seemingly experimental of jazz compositions. As Hughes relates, "jazz to me is one of the inherent expressions of Negro life in America; the eternal tom-tom beating in the Negro soul—the tom-tom of revolt against weariness in a white world, a world of subway trains, and work, work, work; the tom-tom of joy and laughter, and pain swallowed in a smile." Nowhere was this achieved as clearly as in Billie Holiday, who fittingly closes the book in a section called "Muting." Lady Day has inspired some of the best jazz poems, from Langston Hughes' questioning "Song of Billie Holiday" to the beauty and grace of Rita Dove's "Canary" with its often quoted last line: "If you can't be free, be a mystery." Mystery, improvisation, modalities, melody are just some of the ways jazz provides a kind of freedom, not only of a musical but spiritual sort.

At its best, jazz also offers a kind of redemption, evoked in this book's closing poem, "The Journey."

Written by Lawson Fusao Inada, it is a fine poem by a poet too often overlooked—not only is he the first Asian American poet published in the States, but he has consistently written about jazz (and about meeting Lady Day and other jazz figures). His poem, picturing an afterlife of music, is one that the blues may not often invoke but that jazz seems to require and insist upon. Soaring in a spiritual, moaning like the blues, rolling along like justice or the rock'n'roll it inspired, jazz challenges us to hear the world anew, even though, Billie Holiday sang, it "don't explain."

Kevin Young

VAMPING

Early Jazz Poems

If you have to ask,
you'll never know.

LOUIS ARMSTRONG
when asked to define jazz

JAZZONIA

Oh, silver tree!
Oh, shining rivers of the soul!

In a Harlem cabaret
Six long-headed jazzers play.
A dancing girl whose eyes are bold
Lifts high a dress of silken gold.

Oh, singing tree!
Oh, shining rivers of the soul!

Were Eve's eyes
In the first garden
Just a bit too bold?
Was Cleopatra gorgeous
In a gown of gold?

Oh, shining tree!
Oh, silver rivers of the soul!

In a whirling cabaret
Six long-headed jazzers play.

JAZZ BAND IN A
PARISIAN CABARET

Play that thing,
Jazz band!
Play it for the lords and ladies,
For the dukes and counts,
For the whores and gigolos,
For the American millionaires,
And the school teachers
Out for a spree.
Play it,
Jazz band!
You know that tune
That laughs and cries at the same time.
You know it.

   May I?
   Mais oui.
   Mein Gott!
   Parece una rumba.
Play it, jazz band!
You've got seven languages to speak in
And then some,
Even if you do come from Georgia.
   Can I go home wid yuh, sweetie?
   Sure.

THE CAT AND THE SAXOPHONE (2 A.M.)

EVERYBODY
Half-pint,—
Gin?
No, make it
LOVES MY BABY
corn. You like
liquor,
don't you, honey?
BUT MY BABY
Sure. Kiss me,
DON'T LOVE NOBODY
daddy.
BUT ME.
Say!
EVERYBODY
Yes?
WANTS MY BABY
I'm your
BUT MY BABY
sweetie, ain't I?
DON'T WANT NOBODY
Sure.
BUT
Then let's

ME,
do it!
SWEET ME.
Charleston,
mamma!
!

TRUMPET PLAYER

The Negro
With the trumpet at his lips
Has dark moons of weariness
Beneath his eyes
Where the smoldering memory
Of slave ships
Blazed to the crack of whips
About his thighs.

The Negro
With the trumpet at his lips
Has a head of vibrant hair
Tamed down,
Patent-leathered now
Until it gleams
Like jet—
Were jet a crown.

The music
From the trumpet at his lips
Is honey
Mixed with liquid fire.
The rhythm
From the trumpet at his lips
Is ecstasy
Distilled from old desire—

Desire
That is longing for the moon
Where the moonlight's but a spotlight
In his eyes,
Desire
That is longing for the sea
Where the sea's a bar-glass
Sucker size.

The Negro
With the trumpet at his lips
Whose jacket
Has a *fine* one-button roll,
Does not know
Upon what riff the music slips
Its hypodermic needle
To his soul—

But softly
As the tune comes from his throat
Trouble
Mellows to a golden note.

JAZZ FANTASIA

Drum on your drums, batter on your banjoes,
sob on the long cool winding saxophones.
Go to it, O jazzmen.

Sling your knuckles on the bottoms of the happy
tin pans, let your trombones ooze, and go husha-
husha-hush with the slippery sand-paper.

Moan like an autumn wind high in the lonesome tree-
tops, moan soft like you wanted somebody terrible, cry
like a racing car slipping away from a motorcycle cop,
bang-bang! you jazzmen, bang altogether drums, traps,
banjoes, horns, tin cans—make two people fight on the
top of a stairway and scratch each other's eyes in a
clinch tumbling down the stairs.

Can the rough stuff...now a Mississippi steamboat
pushes up the night river with a hoo-hoo-hoo-oo...and
the green lanterns calling to the high soft stars...a red
moon rides on the humps of the low river hills...go to
it, O jazzmen.

POEM

Little brown boy,
Slim, dark, big-eyed,
Crooning love songs to your banjo
Down at the Lafayette—
Gee, boy, I love the way you hold your head,
High sort of and a bit to one side,
Like a prince, a jazz prince. And I love
Your eyes flashing, and your hands,
And your patent-leathered feet,
And your shoulders jerking the jig-wa.
And I love your teeth flashing,
And the way your hair shines in the spotlight
Like it was the real stuff.
Gee, brown boy, I loves you all over.
I'm glad I'm a jig. I'm glad I can
Understand your dancin' and your
Singin', and feel all the happiness
And joy and don't-care in you.
Gee, boy, when you sing, I can close my ears
And hear tom-toms just as plain.
Listen to me, will you, what do I know
About tom-toms? But I like the word, sort of,
Don't you? It belongs to us.
Gee, boy, I love the way you hold your head,
And the way you sing and dance,

And everything.
Say, I think you're wonderful. You're
All right with me,
You are.

THE JAZZ OF THIS HOTEL

Why do I curse the jazz of this hotel?
I like the slower tom-toms of the sea;
I like the slower tom-toms of the thunder;
I like the more deliberate dancing knee
Of outdoor love, of outdoor talk and wonder.
I like the slower, deeper violin
Of the wind across the fields of Indian corn;
I like the far more ancient violoncello
Of whittling loafers telling stories mellow
Down at the village grocery in the sun;
I like the slower bells that ring for church
Across the Indiana landscape old.
Therefore I curse the jazz of this hotel
That seems so hot, but is so hard and cold.

"GOD PITY ME WHOM
(GOD DISTINCTLY HAS)"

god pity me whom(god distinctly has)
the weightless svelte drifting sexual feather
of your shall i say body?follows
truly through a dribbling moan of jazz

whose arched occasional steep youth swallows
curvingly the keenness of my hips;
or,your first twitch of crisp boy flesh dips
my height in a firm fragile stinging weather,

(breathless with sharp necessary lips)kid

female cracksman of the nifty,ruffian-rogue,
laughing body with wise breasts half-grown,
lisping flesh quick to thread the fattish drone
of I Want a Doll,
                    wispish-agile feet with slid
steps parting the tousle of saxophonic brogue.

OL' BUNK'S BAND

These are men! the gaunt, unfore-
    sold, the vocal,
blatant, Stand up, stand up! the
    slap of a bass-string.
Pick, ping! The horn, the
    hollow horn
long drawn out, a hound deep
    tone—
Choking, choking! while the
    treble reed
races—alone, ripples, screams
    slow to fast—
to second to first! These are men!

Drum, drum, drum, drum, drum
    drum, drum! the
ancient cry, escaping crapulence
    eats through
transcendent—torn, tears, term
    town, tense,
turns and back off whole, leaps
    up, stomps down,
rips through! These are men
    beneath

whose force the melody limps—
     to
proclaim, proclaims—Run and
     lie down,
in slow measures, to rest and
     not never
need no more! These are men!
     Men!

CABARET

(1927, Black & Tan Chicago)

Rich, flashy, puffy-faced,
Hebrew and Anglo-Saxon,
The overlords sprawl here with their glittering
    darlings.
The smoke curls thick, in the dimmed light
Surreptitiously, deaf-mute waiters
Flatter the grandees,
Going easily over the rich carpets,
Wary lest they kick over the bottles
Under the tables.

The jazzband unleashes its frenzy.

> *Now, now,*
> *To it, Roger; that's a nice doggie,*
> *Show your tricks to the gentlemen.*

The trombone belches, and the saxophone
Wails curdlingly, the cymbals clash,
The drummer twitches in an epileptic fit

> Muddy water
> Round my feet
> Muddy water

The chorus sways in.
The "Creole Beauties from New Orleans"
(By way of Atlanta, Louisville, Washington, Yonkers,
With stop-overs they've used nearly all their lives)
Their creamy skin flushing rose warm.
O, le bal des belles quarterounes!
Their shapely bodies naked save
For tattered pink silk bodices, short velvet tights,
And shining silver-buckled boots;
Red bandannas on their sleek and close-clipped hair;
To bring to mind (aided by the bottles under the tables)
Life upon the river—

    Muddy water, river sweet

(Lafitte the pirate, instead,
And his doughty diggers of gold)

      There's peace and happiness there
      I declare

(In Arkansas,
Poor half-naked fools, tagged with identification numbers,
Worn out upon the levees,

Are carted back to the serfdom
They had never left before
And may never leave again)

Bee—dap—ee—DOOP, dee—ba—dee—BOOP

The girls wiggle and twist

Oh you too,
Proud high-stepping beauties,
Show your paces to the gentlemen.
A prime filly, seh.
What am I offered, gentlemen, gentlemen....

I've been away a year today
To wander and roam
I don't care if it's muddy there

(Now that the floods recede,
What is there left the miserable folk?
Oh time in abundance to count their losses,
There is so little else to count.)

Still it's my home, sweet home

From the lovely throats
Moans and deep cries for home:

Nashville, Toledo, Spout Springs, Boston,
Creoles from Germantown;—
The bodies twist and rock;
The glasses are filled up again....

(In Mississippi
The black folk huddle, mute, uncomprehending,
Wondering "how come the good Lord
Could treat them this a way")

> shelter
> Down in the Delta

(Along the Yazoo
The buzzards fly over, over, low,
Glutted, but with their scrawny necks stretching,
Peering still.)

> I've got my toes turned Dixie ways
> Round that Delta let me laze

The band goes mad, the drummer throws his sticks
At the moon, a *papier-mâché* moon,
The chorus leaps into weird posturings,
The firm-fleshed arms plucking at grapes to stain
Their coralled mouths; seductive bodies weaving
Bending, writhing, turning

My heart cries out for
MUDDY WATER

(Down in the valleys
The stench of the drying mud
Is a bitter reminder of death.)

Dee da dee DAAAAH

BRINGING JAZZ
Odd-numbered lines spoken slowly:
even-numbered ones quickly

Last night I had an oboe dream—
Whistlers in a box-car madness bringing jazz.
Their faces stormed in a hobo-gleam,
Blinding all the grinding wheels and singing jazz.
The box-car gloried in its dirt—
Just a hallelujah made of chanting mud.
And one old bum opened up his shirt,
Showing wounds of music in his ranting blood.
The hoboes sang with scorching notes
Burning up the pain into a gale of jazz,
While sadness poured in their shaking throats,
Like a molten bugle in a wail of jazz.
The rails were jails for death and rust—
Holding up the cruel, dark blue speed of jazz—
But life still stirred underneath their crust—
Little hums and clicks brought by the need of jazz.
Within the box-car, hoboes leaped—
Fatalists and pagans in a carefree trap—
And when they sang of hungers reaped,
Bread and wine of sound came from a dark god's lap!
The hoboes made a fox-trot blaze—
Scorning women, gliding in a sexless dance—
And on their coats of raggèd baize

Ghosts of orchids fluttered down and looked askance!
The jungle sent a moan of sound—
Made it blend into an oath of northern grime.
A music came, flaring and profound,
Flayed with rapture half repelled and half sublime.
And then I saw the dream's dark spring—
Hurricanes of jazz born from the underworld.
"Saint Louie Gal with a diamond ring"
Danced with mobs of hoboes while the thunder
        swirled!

HOMAGE TO LITERATURE

When you imagine trumpet-faced musicians
blowing again inimitable jazz
no art can accuse nor cannonadings hurt,

or coming out of your dreams of dirigibles
again see the unreasonable cripple
throwing his crutch headlong as the headlights

streak down the torn street, as the three hammerers
go One, Two, Three on the stake, triphammer poundings
and not a sign of new worlds to still the heart;

then stare into the lake of sunset as it runs
boiling, over the west past all control
rolling and swamps the heartbeat and repeats
sea beyond sea after unbearable suns;
think: poems fixed this landscape: Blake, Donne, Keats.

JAZZ BAND

Play that thing, you jazz mad fools!
Boil a skyscraper with a jungle
Dish it to 'em sweet and hot—
Ahhhhhhhhh
Rip it open then sew it up, jazz band!

Thick bass notes from a moon faced drum
Saxophones moan, banjo strings hum
High thin notes from the cornet's throat
Trombone snorting, bass horn snorting
Short tan notes from the piano
And the short tan notes from the piano

Plink plank plunk a plunk
Plink plank plunk a plunk
Chopin gone screwy, Wagner with the blues
Plink plank plunk a plunk
Got a date with Satan—ain't no time to lose
Plink plank plunk a plunk
Strut it in Harlem, let Fifth Avenue shake it slow
Plink plank plunk a plunk
Ain't goin' to heaven nohow—
        crowd up there's too slow...
Plink plank plunk a plunk
Plink plank plunk a plunk
Plunk

Do that thing, jazz band!

Whip it to a jelly

Sock it, rock it; heat it, beat it; then fling it at 'em

Let the jazz stuff fall like hail on king and truck driver,
queen and laundress, lord and laborer, banker and
bum

Let it fall in London, Moscow, Paris, Hongkong,
Cairo, Buenos Aires, Chicago, Sydney

Let it rub hard thighs, let it be molten fire in the veins
of dancers

Make 'em shout a crazy jargon of hot hosannas to a
fiddle-faced jazz god

Send Dios, Jehovah, Gott, Allah, Buddha past in a high
stepping cake walk

Do that thing, jazz band!

Your music's been drinking hard liquor
Got shanghaied and it's fightin' mad
Stripped to the waist feedin' ocean liner bellies
Big burly bibulous brute
Poet hands and bone crusher shoulders—
Black sheep or white?

Hey, Hey!
Pick it, papa!
Twee twa twee twa twa
Step on it, black boy
Do re mi fa sol la ti do
Boomp boomp
Play that thing, you jazz mad fools!

WE REAL COOL

THE POOL PLAYERS.
SEVEN AT THE GOLDEN SHOVEL.

We real cool. We
Left school. We

Lurk late. We
Strike straight. We

Sing sin. We
Thin gin. We

Jazz June. We
Die soon.

SWINGING

Jazz Origins, New Orleans, & Ellingtonia

It don't mean a thing
If it ain't got that swing!

DUKE ELLINGTON

TOUCHING THE PAST

Uptown New Orleans, 1940,
And here was a man of the right color,
Old enough to have been there,

Who maybe heard. So I enquired
From the old man doing his yard work,
"Ever hear Buddy Bolden play?"

"Ah me," he said, stopping his work,
"Yes. But you mean *King, King* Bolden.
That's what we called him then."

He leaned on his rake a while, resting.
"Used to play in Algiers, played so loud
We could hear him clear 'cross the river."

He seemed listening. "King Bolden, now,
There was a man could play." We stood there,
Thinking about it, smiling.

THE BUDDY BOLDEN CYLINDER

It doesn't exist, I know, but I love
to think of it, wrapped in a shawl
or bridal veil, or, less dramatically,
in an old copy of the *Daily Picayune*,
and like an unstaled, unhatched egg
from which, at the right touch, like mine,
the legendary tone, sealed these long years
in the amber of neglect, would peal and re-
peal across the waters. What waters do
I have in mind? Nothing symbolic, mind you.
I meant the sinuous and filth-rich
Mississippi across which you could hear
him play from Gretna, his tone was so loud
and sweet, with a moan in it like you were
in church, and on those old, slow, low-down
blues Buddy could make the women jump
the way they liked. But it doesn't exist,
it never did, except as a relic
for a jazz hagiography, and all
we think we know about Bolden's music
is, really, a melancholy gossip
and none of it sown by Bolden, who
spent his last twenty-four years in Jackson
(Insane Asylum of Louisiana)
hearing the voices of people who spooked

him before he got there. There's more than one
kind of ghostly music in the air, all
of them like the wind: you can't see it
but you can see the leaves shiver in place
as if they'd like to turn their insides out.

IN PRAISE OF BUDDY BOLDEN

1. You have shown me dissipation, the tome, the rhythm, and cool sonorous blue...
2. The right consciousness is always dream, it wakes in us ideology and topos.
3. Not only the blues like melic, like persimmon and soda.
4. Not anything, just blonde sorrow.
5. I can't wait to choose my own fall, the bass and pica.
6. Did you taste the drug, the white words of sound...
7. Nothing will prepare me, not even drums and delusion. I wander in their halls, their tantrums. But mine was apparatus and rebellion. The plumb edifice of transgression.
8. When we play, nothing else matters, not the placards on the train, not the yet and the how. We find plums and pendulums.
9. I told them that this was not enough. No horses, no shoulders, no fields to drown, only blank cotton testimony and confession.
10. When we leave, we leave the pipe and parts of the body. You whistle like a factory. Me, like an empty room.

11. I would like to test myself, and remove these old tunings and feathers, these tulips.
12. Do it then. Leave for the salty tincture of the city, the North.
13. The leaves were all cankered when I returned. Like a salvo I burned. Not for them. Not for this place. But for this rotten reflection. The only true rejection of process.
14. You meant to leave the phonetic terror of the moon, the New Orleans horn of sand and distraction.
15. Leave me to fall. For this is all that I know. I accept, I accept this black stone of mine, mine own three lives, my crime.

BLACK AND BLUE
(WHAT DID I DO TO BE SO BLACK AND BLUE?)

VERSE
Out in the street,
Shufflin' feet,
Couples passin' two by two,
While here am I,
Left high and dry,
Black, and 'cause I'm black I'm blue.
Browns and yellers
All have fellers,
Gentlemen prefer them light.
Wish I could fade,
Can't make the grade,
Nothin' but dark days in sight.

REFRAIN 1
Cold empty bed,
Springs hard as lead,
Pains in my head,
Feels like old Ned,
What did I do
To be so black and blue?
No joys for me,
No company,

Even the mouse
Ran from my house,
All my life through
I've been so black and blue.
I'm white
Inside,
It don't help my case,
'Cause I
Can't hide
What is on my face, ooh!
I'm so forlorn,
Life's just a thorn,
My heart is torn,
Why was I born?
What did I do
To be so black and blue?

REFRAIN 2
Just 'cause you're black,
Folks think you lack,
They laugh at you
And scorn you too,
What did I do

To be so black and blue?
When you are near,
They laugh and sneer,
Set you aside
And you're denied;
What did I do
To be so black and blue?
How sad I am,
Each day I feel worse,
My mark of Ham
Seems to be a curse, ooh!
How will it end?
Ain't got a friend,
My only sin
Is in my skin,
What did I do
To be so black and blue?

MUSIC BY THOMAS "FATS" WALLER

LOUIS ARMSTRONG

suddenly in the midst of a game of lotto with his sisters
Armstrong let a roar out of him that he had the raw
    meat
red wet flesh for Louis
and he up and he sliced him two rumplips
since when his trumpet bubbles
their fust buss

poppies burn on the black earth
he weds the flood he lulls her

some of these days muffled in ooze
down down down down
pang of white in my hair

after you're gone
Narcissus lean and slippered

you're driving me crazy and the trumpet
is Ole Bull it chassés aghast
out of the throes of morning
down the giddy catgut
and *confessing* and my woe slavers
the black music it can't be easy
it threshes the old heart into a spin
into a blaze

Louis lil' ole fader Mississippi
his voice gushes into the lake
the rain spouts back into heaven
his arrows from afar they fizz through the wild horses
they fang you and me
then they fly home

flurry of lightning in the earth
sockets for his rootbound song
nights of Harlem scored with his nails
snow black slush when his heart rises

his she-notes they have more tentacles than the sea
they woo me they close my eyes
they suck me out of the world

"JELLY WROTE"

jelly wrote,
> you should be walking on four legs
> but now you're walking on two.
> you know you come directly from the
> animal famulee

& you do. but dr jive
the winding boy, whose hands only work
was music & pushing
"certain ignorant light skin women" to the corner
was never animal

was never beast in storeyville, refining
a touch for ivory on pool green
with the finest of whorehouse ragtime; use even
for the "darker niggers music. rough," jelly wrote
"but they loved it in the tenderloin."

o the tall & chancey, the ladies'
fancy, the finest boy for miles around,
"your salty dog," but with diamond incisors,
shooting the agate under a stetson sky
his st louis flats winked into

aaah, mr jelly

A. B. SPELLMAN   59

THE FANTASTIC NAMES OF JAZZ

Zoot Sims, Joshua Redman,
Billie Holiday, Pete Fountain,
Fats Marable, Ivie Anderson,
Meade Lux Lewis, Mezz Mezzrow,
Manzie Johnson, Marcus Roberts,
Omer Simeon, Miff Mole, Sister
Rosetta Tharpe, Freddie Slack,
Thelonious Monk, Charlie Teagarden,
Max Roach, Paul Celestin, Muggsy
Spanier, Boomie Richman, Panama
Francis, Abdullah Ibrahim, Piano
Red, Champion Jack Dupree,
Cow Cow Davenport, Shirley Horn,
Cedar Walton, Sweets Edison,
Jaki Byard, John Heard, Joy Harjo,
Pinetop Smith, Tricky Sam
Nanton, Major Holley, Stuff Smith,
Bix Beiderbecke, Bunny Berigan,
Mr. Cleanhead Vinson, Ruby Braff,
Cootie Williams, Cab Calloway,
Lockjaw Davis, Chippie Hill,
And of course Jelly Roll Morton.

FOR SIDNEY BECHET

That note you hold, narrowing and rising, shakes
Like New Orleans reflected on the water,
And in all ears appropriate falsehood wakes,

Building for some a legendary Quarter
Of balconies, flower-baskets and quadrilles,
Everyone making love and going shares—

Oh, play that thing! Mute glorious Storyvilles
Others may license, grouping round their chairs
Sporting-house girls like circus tigers (priced

Far above rubies) to pretend their fads,
While scholars *manqués* nod around unnoticed
Wrapped up in personnels like old plaids.

On me your voice falls as they say love should,
Like an enormous yes. My Crescent City
Is where your speech alone is understood,

And greeted as the natural noise of good,
Scattering long-haired grief and scored pity.

BIX BEIDERBECKE (1903–1931)
January, 1926

China Boy. Lazy Daddy. Cryin' All Day.
He dreamed he played the notes so slowly that
they hovered in the air above the crowd
and shimmered like a neon sign. But no,
the club stayed dark, trays clattered in the kitchen,
people drank and went on talking. He watched
the smoke drift from a woman's cigarette
and slowly circle up across the room
until the ceiling fan blades chopped it up.
A face, a young girl's face, looked up at him,
the stupid face of small-town innocence.
He smiled her way and wondered who she was.
He looked again and saw the face was his.

He woke up then. His head still hurt from drinking,
Jimmy was driving. Tram was still asleep.
Where were they anyway? Near Davenport?
There was no distance in these open fields—
only time, time marked by a farmhouse
or a barn, a tin-topped silo or a tree,
some momentary silhouette against
the endless, empty fields of snow.
He lit a cigarette and closed his eyes.
The best years of his life! The Boring 'Twenties.
He watched the morning break across the snow.
Would heaven be as white as Iowa?

"SURE," SAID BENNY GOODMAN,

"We rode out the depression on technique." How
    gratifying, how rare,
Such expressions of a proper modesty. Notice it was
    not said
By T. Dorsey, who could not play a respectable
    "Honeysuckle Rose" on a kazoo,
But by the man who turned the first jazz concert in
    Carnegie Hall
Into an artistic event and put black musicians on the
    stand with white ones equally,
The man who called himself Barefoot Jackson, or some
    such,
In order to be a sideman with Mel Powell on a small
    label
And made good music on "Blue Skies," etc. He knew
    exactly who he was, no more, no less.
It was rare and gratifying, as I've said. Do you
    remember the Incan priestling, Xtlgg, who said,
"O Lord Sun, we are probably not good enough to
    exalt thee," and got himself
Flung over the wall at Machu Picchu for his candor?
I honor him for that, but I like him because his
    statement implies
That if he had foreseen the outcome he might not have
    said it.

But he did say it. *Candor seeks its own unforeseeable*
   occasions.
Once in America in a dark time the existentialist
   flatfoot floogie stomped across the land
Accompanied by a small floy floy. I think we shall not
   see their like in our people's art again.

ROSE SOLITUDE
For Duke Ellington

I am essence of Rose Solitude
my cheeks are laced with cognac
my hips sealed with five satin nails
i carry dreams and romance of new fools and old flames
between the musk of fat
and the side pocket of my mink tongue

Listen to champagne bubble from this solo

Essence of Rose Solitude
veteran from texas tiger from chicago   that's me
i cover the shrine of Duke
who like Satchmo   like Nat (King) Cole
will never die because love they say
never dies

I tell you   from stair steps of these navy blue nights
these metallic snakes
these flashing fish skins
and the melodious cry of Shango
surrounded by sorrow
by purple velvet tears
by cockhounds limping from crosses
from turtle skinned shoes

from diamond shaped skulls and canes
made from dead gazelles
wearing a face of wilting potato plants
of grey and black scissors
of bee bee shots and fifty red boils
yes the whole world loved him

I tell you from suspenders of two-timing dog odors
from inca frosted lips
nonchalant legs
i tell you from howling chant of sister Erzulie
and the exaggerated hearts of a hundred pretty
        women
they loved him
this world sliding from a single flower
into a caravan of heads made into ten thousand
        flowers

Ask me
Essence of Rose Solitude
chickadee from arkansas that's me
i sleep on cotton bones
cotton tails
and mellow myself in empty ballrooms
i'm no fly by night
look at my resume
i walk through the eyes of staring lizards

i throw my neck back to floorshow on bumping goat
        skins
in front of my stage fright
i cover the hands of Duke who like Satchmo
like Nat (King) Cole will never die
because love they say
never dies

LUSH LIFE

I used to visit all the very gay places,
Those come-what-may places,
Where one relaxes on the axis of the wheel of life
To get the feel of life
From jazz and cocktails.
The girls I knew had sad and sullen gray faces,
With distingué traces
That used to be there.
You could see where
They'd been washed away
By too many through the day
Twelve o'clock tails.
Then you came along
With your siren song
To tempt me to madness.
I thought for a while
That your poignant smile
Was tinged with the sadness
Of a great love for me.
Ah, yes, I was wrong,
Again, I was wrong!
Life is lonely again,
And only last year
Ev'rything seemed so sure.
Now life is awful again,

A troughful of hearts could only be a bore.
A week in Paris will ease the bite of it.
All I care is to smile in spite of it.
I'll forget you, I will,
While yet you are still
Burning inside my brain.
Romance is mush, stifling those who strive.
I'll live a lush life in some small dive,
And there I'll be, while I rot with the rest
Of those whose lives are lonely too.

BILLY STRAYHORN WRITES "LUSH LIFE"

Empty ice-cream carton
in a kitchen garbage can.
Up all night with your mother.
He beat her again. Up all night
eating ice-cream, you made your mother laugh.

>   *ly*
> *Life   is lone*

Duke's hands on your shoulders,
you play it again. Cancer
eats moth holes through
you and you and you.

>   *ly*
> *Life   is lone*

Speeding upstate in the backseat,
on the Taconic, cocktail
in one hand, book in another
as autumn leaves blur by.
This life, New York, piano,
love, then lonely, this life, love.

FOUR BONGOS: TAKE A TRAIN
for Vinnie

The drummer wears suspenders to look like
an old-timer, and plays a salsa
"Caravan," bad boy from the panyard with

an evil, evil beat. The conga man
chants Yoruba and shakes his sweat loose on
a girl up front. His hand worries the drum

like a live fish trashing. Call the bassist
"Pops," with his grizzly goatee, his Banshee
yelp, his rhumba step. The hall is fluorescent.

"Take a Train," Lawrence Welk called that tune,
and played. Ellington hovers above this group
like changeable weather, in gabardine.

THE SYNCOPATED CAKEWALK

My present life is a Sunday morning cartoon.
In it, I see Miss Hand and her Five Daughters
rubbing my back and the backs of my legs.
Nat King Cole provides the music and the words.
It's 1949. Finished with them, I take off
on a riverboat, down the Mississippi, looking for work.
On deck they got the Original Dixieland Jazz Band
doing "Big Butter and Egg Man."
A guru has the cabin next to mine and everybody
        who visits him whimpers something terrible!
Stood on deck after dinner watching the clouds
        form faces and arms. The Shadow went
by giggling to himself.
An Illinois Central ticket fell from his pocket.
Snake Hips picked it up, ran.
Texas Shuffle, who sat in with the Band last night,
        this morning, dropped his fiddlecases
in the ocean and did the Lindy all the way
        to the dinning room.
I got off at Freak Lips Harbor.
Boy from Springfield said he'd talk like Satch for me
        for a dime. I gave him a Bird
and an introductory note to the Duke of Ellington.
Found my way to the Ida B. Wells Youth Center.
Girl named Ella said I'd have to wait to see Mister B.

Everybody else was out to lunch.
In the waiting room got into a conversation
      with a horse thief from Jump Back. Told him:
My past life is a Saturday morning cartoon.
In it, I'm jumping Rock Island freight cars, skipping
      Peoria with Leadbelly; running from the man,
trying to prove my innocence. Accused of being
too complex to handle.
Meanwhile, Zoot, Sassy, Getz, Prez, Cootie, everybody
      gives me a hand.
Finally, Mister B comes in. Asks about my future.
All I can say is, I can do the Cow Cow Boogie
      on the ocean and hold my own in a chase chorus
among the best!
Fine, says Mister B, *you start seven in the morning!*

MOOD INDIGO

it hasnt always been this way
ellington was not a street
robeson no mere memory
du bois walked up my father's stairs
hummed some tune over me
sleeping in the company of men
who changed the world

it wasnt always like this
why ray barretto used to be a side-man
& dizzy's hair was not always grey
i remember   i was there
i listened in the company of men
politics as necessary as collards
music even in our dreams

our house was filled with all kinda folks
our windows were not cement or steel
our doors opened like our daddy's arms
held us safe & loved
children growing in the company of men
old southern men & young slick ones
sonny til was not a boy
the clovers no rag-tag orphans
our crooners/ we belonged to a whole world

nkrumah was no foreigner
virgil aikens was not the only fighter

it hasnt always been this way
ellington was not a street

BOP

Bird & Beyond

Oop-pop-a-da!
Skee! Daddle de-do!
Be-bop!

Salt'peanuts!

De-dop!

LANGSTON HUGHES
Montage of a Dream Deferred

WAR MEMOIR

Jazz—listen to it at your own risk.
At the beginning, a warm dark place.

(Her screams were trumpet laughter,
Not quite blues, but almost sinful.)

Crying above the pain, we forgave ourselves;
Original sin seemed a broken record.
God played blues to kill time, all the time.
Red-waved rivers floated us into life.

(So much laughter, concealed by blood and faith;
Life is a saxophone played by death.)

Greedy to please, we learned to cry;
Hungry to live, we learned to die.
The heart is a sad musician,
Forever playing the blues.

The blues blow life, as life blows fright;
Death begins, jazz blows soft in the night,
Too soft for ears of men whose minds
Hear only the sound of death, of war,
Of flagwrapped cremation in bitter lands.

No chords of jazz as mud is shoveled
Into the mouths of men; even the blues shy
At cries of children dying on deserted corners.
Jazz deserted, leaving us to our burning.

(Jazz is an African traitor.)

What one-hundred-percent redblooded savage
Wastes precious time listening to jazz
With so much important killing to do?

Silence the drums, that we may hear the burning
Of Japanese in atomic colorcinemascope,
And remember the stereophonic screaming.

WALKING PARKER HOME

Sweet beats of jazz impaled on slivers of wind
Kansas Black Morning/ First Horn Eyes/
Historical sound pictures on New Bird wings
People shouts/ boy alto dreams/ Tomorrow's
Gold belled pipe of stops and future Blues Times
Lurking Hawkins/ shadows of Lester/ realization
Bronze fingers—brain extensions seeking trapped
    sounds
Ghetto thoughts/ bandstand courage/ solo flight
Nerve-wracked suspicions of newer songs and doubts
New York altar city/ black tears/ secret disciples
Hammer horn pounding soul marks on unswinging
    gates
Culture gods/ mob sounds/ visions of spikes
Panic excursions to tribal Jazz wombs and transfusions
Heroin nights of birth/ and soaring/ over boppy new
    ground.
Smothered rage covering pyramids of notes
    spontaneously exploding
Cool revelations/ shrill hopes/ beauty speared into
    greedy ears
Birdland nights on bop mountains, windy saxophone
    revolutions.
Dayrooms of junk/ and melting walls and circling
    vultures/

81

Money cancer/ remembered pain/ terror flights/
Death and indestructible existence

In that Jazz corner of life
Wrapped in a mist of sound
His legacy, our Jazz-tinted dawn
Wailing his triumphs of oddly begotten dreams
Inviting the nerveless to feel once more
That fierce dying of humans consumed
In raging fires of Love.

CROOTEY SONGO

DERRAT SLEGELATIONS, FLO GOOF BABER,
SCRASH SHO DUBIES, WAGO WAILO WAILO.
GEED BOP NAVA GLIED, NAVA GLIED NAVA,
SPLEERIEDER, HUYEDIST, HEDACAZ, AX——, O, O.

DEEREDITION, BOOMEDITION, SQUOM, SQUOM, SQUOM.
DEE BEETSTRAWIST, WAPAGO, LOCOEST, LOCORO, LO.
VOOMETEYEREEPETIOP, BOP, BOP, BOP, WHIPOLAT.

DEGET, SKLOKO, KURRITIF, PLOG, MANGI, PLOG MANGI,
CLOPO JAGO BREE, BREE, ASLOOPERED, AKINGO LABY.
ENGPOP, ENGPOP, BOP, PLOLO, PLOLO, BOP, BOP.

ELEVEN
From *Velvet Bebop Kente Cloth*

There ain't/No word
I ain't/Heard.
ain't/No word
Bird/Ain't heard.

Language is an/Inventor's
privilege.

I/Blow psalms.
I/Blow sinners'deeds.
I/Blow prayer before death.
I/Blow curses.
I/Blow laughter.
I/Blow vocabulary of my axe.

You can't/Hold
folks/Down who Be-Bop
but you/Kin hold
them/Up.

Every Be-Bopper/Renew
his/Subscriptions
to/Genius when he riff some
thing/New on his axe.

CHARLES PARKER, 1920–1955

Listen,
This here
Is what
Charlie
Did
To the Blues.
Listen,
That there
Is what
Charlie
Did
To the Blues.
This here,
bid-dle-dee-dee
bid-dle-dee-dee
bopsheep
have you any cool?
bahdada
one horn full.
Charlie
Filled the Blues
With
Curly-cues.
That's what
Charlie

Did
To the Blues.
Play
That again
Drop
A nickel in,
Charlie's
Dead,
Charlie's
Gone,
But
John Birks
Carried on.
Drop
A nickel in,
Give
The platter
A spin,
Let's listen
To what
Charlie
Did
To the Blues.

MAY 12
From *The Daily Mirror*

A book could be written
on the moment swing turned
into bop the moment Lester
Young, Roy Eldridge, and
Teddy Wilson gave way to
Bird, Dizzy, Miles, Bud,
and Monk in fact it would
be a great movie at least
the sound track would be
"beyond category" as Duke
Ellington would have put it
the life of a jazz musician
(about which I know so little)
is the life for me I felt
on the afternoon Jamie and I
visited his father who sat
at the piano and talked and
played I was tongue-tied and
wanted him to play a song
as if Helen Merrill were there
and her voice and his fingers were
about to have an intimate talk

YARDBIRD'S SKULL
For Charlie Parker

The bird is lost,
Dead, with all the music:
Whole sunsets heard the brain's music
Faded to last horizon notes.
I do not know why I hold
This skull, smaller than a walnut's,
Against my ear,
Expecting to hear
The smashed fear
Of childhood from ... bone;
Expecting to see
Wind nosing red and purple,
Strange gold and magic
On bubbled windowpanes
Of childhood. Shall I hear?
I should hear: this skull
Has been with violets
Not Yorick, or the gravedigger,
Yapping his yelling story,
This skull has been in air,
Sensed his brother, the swallow,
(Its talent for snow and crumbs).
Flown to lost Atlantis islands,
Places of dreaming, swimming lemmings.

O I shall hear skull skull,
Hear your lame music,
Believe music rejects undertaking,
Limps back.
Remember tiny lasting, we get lonely:
Come sing, come sing, come sing sing
And sing.

CHASING THE BIRD

The sun sets unevenly and the people
go to bed.

The night has a thousand eyes.
The clouds are low, overhead.

Every night it is a little bit
more difficult, a little

harder. My mind
to me a mangle is.

CHARLIE PARKER BIRTHDAY
CELEBRATION, TOMPKINS SQUARE PARK

I was telling you about that junkie wannabe
from Wall Street who OD'ed last week
on Explosion 2000 on that street corner
right over there when KABOOM! You kissed me
smack on the lips just as "Confirmation" kicked in.
Just as Venus in two-toned dreadlocks and a skin-tight
smock danced from the band shell with her pet python,
Bodyguard, to "All the Things You Are."
Just as punk rockers rocked, in-flowered on sheets,
sipped smoothies and smoked,
their hair spirited to pastel auras, rosehip,
island lime, a shade of blue just washed by rain.
Just as Ukraines checkmated, as twins seesawed,
as bikers cracked smiles in the Hari-Hari, the slap-
tongue of sax. At the mommies and the poppies. Just as.
And they were doing the brothers in descending order.
The three brothers Heath: Percy, Jimmy, call him
        "Little Bird,"
and Albert "Tootie" Heath. With Milt Jackson on vibes,
three score and twelve, and still working. Two boys
        in love
grooved, one in white pants and sailor hat,
the other in a buffalo nickel belt that bedazzled.
They sat on the park bench eating falafel.

A man with one leg sold charms for a dollar. For luck.
For the music that day and the light, you could say it
        was all
bell-bottomed and swaybacked. Young-like.
And your kiss. All at once I was riding a sparkling
        gold Schwinn bike.
Something in my head went from full torpor to starburst:
as if whetted by some wild vibrato, your kiss,
the vibes' licks cleared my vision of fizz for an instant.
What had been all Midnight Dragon was now
a Tropicana-Pure- Premium-sharpened C
delivered as of this morning to the Santa Barbara Deli
and Superetti down the street. Just like that.
In your arms and the music and the light, I thought
        I might
go plumb or Pentecostal, lay down on the grass, recite
Kahlil, take up knitting, eat pickles and marry you—
Tell that priest to stop playing Frisbee with the lab
so we can say our vows right here and now before
        "Tenor Madness"
ends! Oops! I forgot we're already married! Just as.

CHARLIE PARKER: ALMOST LIKE BEING IN LOVE

These are the shadows of water when water
is thick and no longer transparent.
They are everywhere—on the walls,
across the ceiling.

It was always this good.
One night you undressed me in my sleep.
Very slowly, you told me later.
You said I smelled good.
The sweater, I said. I'd taken it
out of the drawer where I kept
my winter clothes.
It smelled of pine and a long summer.
No, you said. Not wood.
More like the inside of a saxophone case,
all velvet and sweet regrets.
All blues, I said. Blues
and whatever shadows are made of,

I said, falling on you like slow water.

PARKER'S MOOD

Come with me,
If you want to go to Kansas City.

I'm feeling lowdown and blue,
My heart's full of sorrow.

Don't hardly know what to do.
Where will I be tomorrow?

Going to Kansas City.
Want to go too?
No, you can't make it with me.
Going to Kansas City,
Sorry that I can't take you.

When you see me coming,
Raise your window high.
When you see me leaving, baby,
Hang your head and cry.

I'm afraid there's nothing in this cream, this
        dreamy town
A honky-tonky monkey-woman can do.
She'd only bring herself down.

So long everybody!
The time has come
And I must leave you
So if I don't ever see your smiling face again:
Make a promise you'll remember
Like a Christmas Day in December
That I told you
All through thick and thin
On up until the end
Parker's been your friend.

Don't hang your head
When you see, when you see those six pretty horses
     pulling me.
Put a twenty dollar silver-piece on my watchchain,
Look at the smile on my face,
And sing a little song
To let the world know I'm really free.
Don't cry for me,
'Cause I'm going to Kansas City.

Come with me,
If you want to go to Kansas City.

KING PLEASURE (CLARENCE BEEKS)   95

VICTROLA

Dead forty years Bird brings his lips to the reed.
He rules the roost, and rues the rest,
Do wot-jadda bop.

Recovered from shell shock
The war veteran Hitler found the doctor
Who cured his hysterical deafness,

And had the man killed, hoping that I
Might never exist to tell the story here,
A little distorted.

But Illinois Jacquet playing *'Round Midnight*
On the bassoon, better even
Than the death speech of Falstaff.

And listen, Moshe Leib Halpern, I
Have a miracle cabinet
Made in Japan—listen.

FILLING THE GAP

When Bird died, I didn't mind:
I had things to do—

polish some shoes, practice
a high school cha-cha-cha.

I didn't even know
Clifford was dead:

I must have been
lobbing an oblong ball
beside the gymnasium.

I saw the Lady
right before she died—

dried, brittle
as last year's gardenia.

I let her scratch an autograph.

But not Pres.

Too bugged to boo, I left
as Basie's brass

booted him off the stand
in a sick reunion—

tottering, saxophone
dragging him like a stage-hook.

When I read Dr. Williams'
poem, "Stormy,"
I wrote a letter of love and praise

and didn't mail it.

After he died, it burned my desk
like a delinquent prescription...

I don't like to mourn the dead:
what didn't, never will.

And I sometimes feel foolish
staying up late,
trying to squeeze some life
out of books and records,
filling the gaps
between words and notes.

That is why
I rush into our room to find you
mumbling and moaning
in your incoherent performance.

That is why
I rub and squeeze you
and love to hear your
live, alterable cry against my breast.

HORN SECTION

JAZZ

It started with an alto horn, and a young
boy who'd grown faster than he should have, and
who'd become great before he should have, and
who sought for the source of the feeling deep in-
side before he should have. He stood in his room
and started with a short burst of notes, and then
sought the tone he'd felt inside him, but which
he couldn't match he couldn't match by blowing.
He blew, fast, and beautifully; seeking the right
burst of notes, notes blown so fast that only God's
perfection would be a match for it. He tried for
a tone that he'd never heard, but which he knew
as a sensation of mystery, of greatness, a feeling
that he was bigger than he seemed to be, could
blow faster than his fingers were letting him,
could cry out the tone that cried within him. All
this strained inside him, strained and drove him,
pushed him and made him whip his fingers upon
the valves of his horn until they hurt. And his
lungs seemed to bleed inside; his eyes ran water,
and he kept blowing, and blowing, with his eyes
closed to the white of the daytime and the touch
of the wind and the sound of the fists banging
at the door, and the bark of the voices outside
his door, shouting: "Open up! It's the police!
What's going on in there?"

FRANK LONDON BROWN

JAZZ IS MY RELIGION

Jazz is my religion   and it alone do I dig   the jazz
clubs are my houses of worship   and sometimes the
concert halls   but some holy places are too commercial
(like churches)   so I dont dig the sermons there   I buy
jazz sides to dig in solitude   Like man/Harlem,
Harlem U.S.A. used to be a jazz heaven where most of
the jazz sermons were preached   but now-a-days due
to chacha cha and rotten rock'n'roll alotta good
jazzmen have sold their souls   but jazz is still my
religion   because I know and feel the message it brings
like Reverend Dizzy Gillespie/ Brother   Bird and
Basie/ Uncle Armstrong/ Minister Monk/ Deacon
Miles Davis/ Rector Rollins/ Priest Ellington/ His
Funkness Horace Silver/ and the great Pope John, John
COLTRANE   and Cecil Taylor   They Preach A
Sermon That Always Swings!!   Yeah jazz is MY
religion   Jazz is my story it was my mom's and
pop's   and their moms and pops from the days of
Buddy Bolden who swung them blues to Charlie Parker
and Ornette Coleman's extension of Bebop   Yeah jazz
is my religion   Jazz is a unique musical religion   the
sermons spread happiness and joy   to be able to dig
and swing inside   what a wonderful feeling jazz is/
YEAH BOY!!   JAZZ is my religion and dig this:
it wasnt for us to choose because they created it for

a damn good reason   as   a weapon to battle our blues!
JAZZ is my religion   and its international   all the
way   JAZZ is just an Afroamerican music and like us
its here to stay   So remember that JAZZ is my religion
but it can be your religion too but JAZZ is a truth
that   is always black and blue   Hallelujah I love JAZZ
so   Hallelujah I dig JAZZ so   Yeah JAZZ   IS
MY   RELIGION

LESTER YOUNG

Sometimes he was cool like an eternal
    blue flame burning in the old Kansas
    City nunnery
Sometimes he was happy 'til he'd think
    about his birth place and its blood
    stained clay hills and crow-filled trees
Most times he was blowin' on the wonderful
    tenor sax of his, preachin' in very cool
    tones, shouting only to remind you of
    a certain point in his blue messages
He was our president as well as the minister
    of soul stirring Jazz, he knew what he
    blew, and he did what a prez should do,
    wail, wail, wail. There were many of
    them to follow him and most of them were
    fair—but they never spoke so eloquently
    in so a far out funky air.
Our prez done died, he know'd this would come
    but death has only booked him, alongside
    Bird, Art Tatum, and other heavenly wailers.
Angels of Jazz—they don't die—they live
they live—in hipsters like you and I

STRING OF PEARLS

Lester Young! why are you playing that clarinet
you know you are Horn in my head? the middle page is
missing god damn it now how will I ever understand
    Nature
And New Painting? doo doot doo Where is
    Dick Gallup
his room is horrible it has books in it and paint peeling
a 1934 icebox living on the fifth floor it's
ridiculous

       yes and it's ridiculous to be sitting here
in New York City 28 years old wife sleeping and
Lester playing the wrong sound in 1936 in
    Kansas City (of
all places) sounding like Benny Goodman (of all
    people) but
a good sound, not a surprise, a voice, & where was
    Billie, he
hadn't met her yet, I guess Gallup wasn't born yet
    neither was
my wife Just me & that icebox I hadn't read HORN
    by John
Clellon Holmes yet, either

What is rhythm I wonder? Which was George &
 which Ira Gershwin? Why
don't I do more? wanting only to be walking in the
 New York Autumn
warm from coffee I still can feel gurgling under my ribs
climbing the steps of the only major statement in
 New York City
(Louis Sullivan) thinking the poem I am going to
 write seeing
the fountains come on wishing I were he

PRES SPOKE IN A LANGUAGE

Pres
    spoke in a language
"of his own." What did he say, between the
horn line
s, pork pie hat
tenor tilted
pres once was a drummer but gave it up cause other
    dudes was getting
the foxes
while he packed his tomtoms
"Ding Dong," pres sd, meaning
like a typewriter, its the end
of this
line. "No Eyes," pres wd say, meaning
I didn't cdn't dig it, and what it was was
lame. Pres
had a language
and a life, like,
all his own,
but in the teeming whole of us he lived
toooting on his sideways horn
translating frankie trumbauer into
Bird's feathers
Tranes sinewy tracks
the slickster walking through the crowd

surviving on a terrifying wit
its the jungle the jungle the jungle
we living in
and cats like pres cd make it because they were clear
    they, at least,
had to,
to do anything else.
Save all that comrades, we need it.

PREZ IN PARIS, 1959

By 1959 he'd moved to Paris.
Prez wouldn't eat. Sweet alcohol harassed
his system. Cooled, the jazz "To Be or Not
to Be"—withdrawn, a whisper—seemed a jot.

Once there'd been ways to get back at the world;
Ex-G.I. Prez had tried and tired. He hurled
himself now—hearsay, smoky horn—down-stage.
"Well, Lady Gay Paree, it's been a dog's age,"

he might've said. Or "Ivy Divey! Wrong!
The way that channel swims—too cold. This song
—the lyric's weak. We'll drown. No eyes, my man.
No, let's don't take it from no top. The band

can skip it." Prez. Monsieur le Président,
who played us what can work, and what just won't.

PERSONAL POEM

Now when I walk around at lunchtime
I have only two charms in my pocket
an old Roman coin Mike Kanemitsu gave me
and a bolt-head that broke off a packing case
when I was in Madrid the others never
brought me too much luck though they did
help keep me in New York against coercion
but now I'm happy for a time and interested

I walk through the luminous humidity
passing the House of Seagram with its wet
and its loungers and the construction to
the left that closed the sidewalk if
I ever get to be a construction worker
I'd like to have a silver hat please
and get to Moriarty's where I wait for
LeRoi and hear who wants to be a mover and
shaker the last five years my batting average
is .016 that's that, and LeRoi comes in
and tells me Miles Davis was clubbed 12
times last night outside BIRDLAND by a cop
a lady asks us for a nickel for a terrible
disease but we don't give her one we
don't like terrible diseases, then

we go eat some fish and some ale it's
cool but crowded we don't like Lionel Trilling
we decide, we like Don Allen we don't like
Henry James so much we like Herman Melville
we don't want to be in the poets' walk in
San Francisco even we just want to be rich
and walk on girders in our silver hats
I wonder if one person out of the 8,000,000 is
thinking of me as I shake hands with LeRoi
and buy a strap for my wristwatch and go
back to work happy at the thought possibly so

FOR MILES

Your sound is faultless
        pure & round
                holy
        almost profound

Your sound is your sound
        true & from within
        a confession
        soulful & lovely

Poet whose sound is played
        lost or recorded
        but heard
        can you recall that 54 night at the Open Door
        when you & bird
        wailed five in the morning some wondrous
        yet unimaginable score?

BLUE IN GREEN

Miles' muted horn penetrates
like liquid, melancholy medicine
to the pinched nerve
of an old misery. I'd hit
the winning shot at State that night;
teary-eyed, Tina kissed me—
way past any doubt, then
wore distance like
a torn red dress the next day.

I feel the rend again—in the piano,
I hear her long, practiced excuses
in Coltrane's troubling tenor—
mixed with this loneliness
I'd felt at seventeen, standing
between rusted railroad tracks
in July.

I turn the lights off—
they go black.

Spare, midnight tones tug at me,
I lean back hard into the past:
I see that winning shot go in,
I see her run at me, again,

and for a moment—she's there
mingled in Coltrane's tenor.
What if

I never get past this pain,
just then Miles wavers back in
with an antidote—
traying eights behind
the ivorys. It works
this time, if I only knew
how it means.

THE BLUES OF THIS DAY
for Miles Davis

The blues of this day
are as elegant and as sad
as minor thirds and we all try to sing it.

What we want is to be brass.
The horn-scratched voice blown through.
Valves as golden as his. Lord as crazy sex
or first real heartbreak.

It was always his back slightly bent away
from all of us who adored him, gazing across his

shoulders as the band jumped into the party
one solo at a time.
Or they could be rocking way off-key
going as far away from the melody as Venus to Mars.
Funk can be as easy as that
getting together in the dark.

And as hard as the breaking light
that catches the throat of sated lovers, the morning after.
The talk the night before by the last of hip men
who knew the way of the world and then some,
about Miles and his two steps ahead of the century

like the first Black man to leave the Delta humming
I gotta go, but I can't take you.
I gotta go, but I can't take you.
If you want to follow, then do what you want to do.

MELODY FORENSIC

If somebody told me I had only one hour to live,
I'd spend it choking a white man. I'd do it nice and slow.
MILES DAVIS

Years in the gristle of knuckles. Thick muscle
at the palm's base. Fingers squeezing,
digging valve keys to mold exhales. Some pain
pinched by the reed—would it wail
if you had found a pink neck before leadpipe brass?
Forgive the epigraph. Don't apologize,
your music may taste funny to someone
after reading this. But damn Miles (if I can call you
Miles) why do black men have to scream in art?
What wants off our tongue floats
in the same ether lungs feed wood-wind
(now you got me doing it). Listen
if "I hurt" falls deaf on their ears,
Kind of Blue is no different.
The black-sound congeals in mason jars
lined across the tops of rickety stoves.
We been frying our story, over-seasoned
with silences. Miles (I'm calling
you Miles) you don't want to play. Sweet indulgence—
let's pretend we're back at the Five Spot, this poem
just another stage light. Move it,

put the trumpet down. Where would you start?
Maybe there, Mr. Cool at the bar—head lolling,
eyes wilted from your blow,
a coil of saliva in his throat so
sure he can swallow your blue note whole.

ALMOST BLUE
Chet Baker, 1929–1988

If Hart Crane played trumpet
he'd sound like you, your horn's dark city

miraculous and broken over and over,
scale-shimmered, every harbor-flung hour

and salt-span of cabled longing,
every waterfront, the night-lovers' rendezvous.

This is the entrance
to the city of you, sleep's hellgate,

and two weeks before the casual relinquishment
of your hold—light needling

on the canal's gleaming haze
and the buds blaring like horns—

two weeks before the end, Chet,
and you're playing like anything,

singing *stay little valentine*
stay

and taking so long there are worlds sinking
between the notes, this exhalation

no longer a voice but a rush of air,
brutal, from the tunnels under the river,

the barges' late whistles you only hear
when the traffic's stilled

by snow, a city hushed and
distilled into one rush of breath,

yours, into the microphone
and the ear of that girl

in the leopard-print scarf,
one long kiss begun on the highway

and carried on dangerously,
the Thunderbird veering

on the coast road: glamor
of a perfectly splayed fender,

dazzling lipstick, a little pearl of junk,
some stretch of road breathless

and traveled into ... Whoever she is
she's the other coast of you,

and just beyond the bridge the city's
long amalgam of ardor and indifference

is lit like a votive
then blown out. Too many rooms unrented

in this residential hotel,
and you don't want to know

why they're making that noise in the hall;
you're going to wake up in any one of the

how many ten thousand
locations of trouble and longing

going out of business forever everything must go
wake up and start wanting.

It's so much better when you don't want:
nothing falls then, nothing lost

but sleep and who wanted that
in the pearl this suspended world is,

in the warm suspension and glaze
of this song everything stays up

almost forever in the long
glide sung into the vein,

one note held almost impossibly
almost blue and the lyric takes so long

to open, a little blood
blooming: *there's no love song   finer*

*but how strange the change
from major to minor*

*everytime
we say goodbye*

and you leaning into that warm
haze from the window, Amsterdam,

late afternoon glimmer
a blur of buds

breathing in the lindens
and you let go and why not

ART PEPPER

It's the broken phrases, the fury inside him.
Squiggling alto saxophone playing out rickets
And jaundice, a mother who tried to kill him
In her womb with a coat hanger, a faltering
God-like father. The past is a bruised cloud
Floating over the houses like a prophecy,
The terrible foghorns off the shore at San Pedro.

Lightning without thunder. Years without playing.
Years of blowing out smoke and inhaling fire,
Junk and cold turkey, smacking up, the habit
Of cooking powder in spoons, the eyedroppers,
The spikes. Tracks on both arms. Tattoos.
The hospital cells at Fort Worth, the wire cages
In the L.A. County, the hole at San Quentin.

And always the blunt instrument of sex, the pain
Bubbling up inside him like a wound, the small
Deaths. The wind piercing the sheer skin
Of a dark lake at dawn. The streets at 5 a.m.
After a cool rain. The smoky blue clubs.
The chords of Parker, of Young, of Coltrane.
Playing solo means going on alone, improvising,

Hitting the notes, ringing the changes.
It's clipped phrasing and dry ice in summer,
Straining against the rhythm, speeding it up,
Loping forward and looping back, finding the curl
In the wave, the mood in the air. It's
Splintered tones and furious double timing.
It's leaving the other instruments on stage

And blowing freedom into the night, into the faces
Of emptiness that peer along the bar, ghosts,
Shallow hulls of nothingness. Hatred of God.
Hatred of white skin that never turns black.
Hatred of Patti, of Dianne, of Christine.
A daughter who grew up without him, a stranger.
Years of being strung out, years without speaking.

Pauses and intervals, silence. A fog rolling
Across the ocean, foghorns in the distance.
A lighthouse rising from the underworld.
A moon swelling in the clouds, an informer,
A twisted white mouth of light. Scars carved
And crisscrossed on his chest. The memory
Of nodding out, the dazed drop-off into sleep.

And then the curious joy of surviving, joy
Of waking up in a dusky room to a gush
Of fresh notes, a tremoring sheet of sound.

Jamming again. Careening through the scales
For the creatures who haunt the night.
Bopping through the streets in a half-light
With Laurie on his arm, a witness, a believer.

The night is going to burst inside him.
The wind is going to break loose forever
From his lungs. It's the fury of improvising,
Of going on alone. It's the fierce clarity
Of each note coming to an end, distinct,
Glistening. The alto's full-bodied laughter.
The white grief-stricken wail.

SNAKE-BACK SOLO
For Louis Armstrong, Steve Cannon, Miles Davis
& Eugene Redmond

with the music up high
boogalooin bass down way way low
up & under eye come slidin on in mojoin
on in spacin on in on a riff
full of rain
riffin on in full of rain & pain
spacin on in on a sound like coltrane

my metaphor is a blues
hot pain dealin blues is a blues axin
guitar voices whiskey broken niggah deep
in the heart is a blues in a glass filled with rain
is a blues in the dark
slurred voices of straight bourbon
is a blues dagger stuck off in the heart
of night moanin like bessie smith
is a blues filling up the wings
of darkness is a blues

& looking through the heart
a dream can become a raindrop window to see through
can become a window to see through this moment
to see yourself hanging around the dark
to see through
can become a river catching rain
feeding time can become a window
to see through

BODY AND SOUL II
For Coleman Hawkins

The structure of landscape is infinitesimal,
Like the structure of music,

                                    seamless, invisible.
Even the rain has larger sutures.
What holds the landscape together, and what holds
        music together,
Is faith, it appears—faith of the eye, faith of the ear.
Nothing like that in language,
However, clouds chugging from west to east like
        blossoms
Blown by the wind.

                            April, and anything's possible.

Here is the story of Hsuan Tsang.
A Buddhist monk, he went from Xian to southern India
And back—on horseback, on camel-back, on
        elephant-back, and on foot.
Ten thousand miles it took him, from 629 to 645,
Mountains and deserts,
In search of the Truth,

                            the heart of the heart of Reality,
The Law that would help him escape it,
And all its attendant and inescapable suffering.

                                        And he found it.

These days, I look at things, not through them,
And sit down low, as far away from the sky as I can get.
The reef of the weeping cherry flourishes coral,
The neighbor's back porch lightbulbs glow like
        anemones.
Squid-eyed Venus floats forth overhead.
This is the half hour, half-light, half-dark,
                        when everything starts to shine out,
And aphorisms skulk in the trees,
Their wings folded, their heads bowed.

Every true poem is a spark,
        and aspires to the condition of the original fire
Arising out of the emptiness.
It is that same emptiness it wants to reignite.
It is that same engendering it wants to be
        re-engendered by.
Shooting stars.
April's identical,
                celestial, wordless, burning down.
Its light is the light we commune by.
Its destination's our own, its hope is the hope we
        live with.

Wang Wei, on the other hand,
Before he was 30 years old bought his famous estate on
    the Wang River
Just east of the east end of the Southern Mountains,
                           and lived there,
Off and on, for the rest of his life.
He never travelled the landscape, but stayed inside it,
A part of nature himself, he thought.
And who would say no
To someone so bound up in solitude,
                in failure, he thought, and suffering.

Afternoon sky the color of Cream of Wheat, a small
Dollop of butter hazily at the western edge.
Getting too old and lazy to write poems,
                     I watch the snowfall
From the apple trees.
Landscape, as Wang Wei says, softens the sharp edges
    of isolation.
Don't just do something, sit there.
And so I have, so I have,
            the seasons curling around me like smoke,
Gone to the end of the earth and back without a sound.

LISTENING TO SONNY ROLLINS
AT THE FIVE SPOT

There will be many other nights like
be standing here with someone, some
one
someone
some-one
some
some
some
some
some
some
one
there will be other songs
a-nother fall, another—spring, but
there will never be a-noth, noth
anoth
noth
anoth-er
noth-er
noth-er
      Other lips that I may kiss,
but they won't thrill me like
         thrill me like
               like yours

used to
        dream a million dreams
but how can they come
when there
            never be
a-noth—

FEBRUARY IN SYDNEY

Dexter Gordon's tenor sax
plays "April in Paris"
inside my head all the way back
on the bus from Double Bay.
Round Midnight, the '50s,
cool cobblestone streets
resound footsteps of Bebop
musicians with whiskey-laced voices
from a boundless dream in French.
Bud, Prez, Webster, & The Hawk,
their names run together riffs.
Painful gods jive talk through
bloodstained reeds & shiny brass
where music is an anesthetic.
Unreadable faces from the human void
float like torn pages across the bus
windows. An old anger drips into my throat,
& I try thinking something good,
letting the precious bad
settle to the salty bottom.
Another scene keeps repeating itself:
I emerge from the dark theatre,
passing a woman who grabs her red purse
& hugs it to her like a heart attack.
Tremolo. Dexter comes back to rest

behind my eyelids. A loneliness
lingers like a silver needle
under my black skin,
as I try to feel how it is
to scream for help through a horn.

SHEETS OF SOUND

Coltrane & Co.

ALONE

A friend told me
He'd risen above jazz.
I leave him there.

MICHAEL S. HARPER

JOHN COLTRANE
an impartial review

may he have new life like the fall
fallen tree, wet moist rotten enough
to see shoots stalks branches & green
leaves (& may the roots) grow into his side.

around the back of the mind, in its closet
is a string, i think, a coil around things.
listen to *summertime*, think of spring, negroes
cats in the closet, anything that makes a rock

of your eye. imagine you steal. you are frightened
you want help. you are sorry you are born with ears.

A. B. SPELLMAN   139

DEAR JOHN, DEAR COLTRANE

a love supreme, a love supreme
a love supreme, a love supreme

Sex fingers toes
in the marketplace
near your father's church
in Hamlet, North Carolina—
witness to this love
in this calm fallow
of these minds,
there is no substitute for pain:
genitals gone or going,
seed burned out,
you tuck the roots in the earth,
turn back, and move
by river through the swamps,
singing: *a love supreme, a love supreme*;
what does it all mean?
Loss, so great each black
woman expects your failure
in mute change, the seed gone.
You plod up into the electric city—
your song now crystal and
the blues. You pick up the horn
with some will and blow

into the freezing night:
a love supreme, a love supreme—

Dawn comes and you cook
up the thick sin 'tween
impotence and death, fuel
the tenor sax cannibal
heart, genitals, and sweat
that makes you clean—
a love supreme, a love supreme—

Why you so black?
cause I am
why you so funky?
cause I am
why you so black?
cause I am
why you so sweet?
cause I am
why you so black?
cause I am
a love supreme, a love supreme:

So sick
you couldn't play *Naima*,
so flat we ached
for song you'd concealed
with your own blood,
your diseased liver gave
out its purity,
the inflated heart
pumps out, the tenor kiss,
tenor love:
a love supreme, a love supreme—
a love supreme, a love supreme—

HERE WHERE COLTRANE IS

Soul and race
are private dominions,
memories and modal
songs, a tenor blossoming,
which would paint suffering
a clear color, but is not in
this Victorian house
without oil in zero degree
weather and a forty-mile-an-hour wind;
it is all a well-knit family:
a love supreme.
Oak leaves pile up on walkway
and steps, catholic as apples
in a special mist of clear white
children who love my children.
I play "Alabama"
on a warped record player
skipping the scratches
on your faces over the fibrous
conical hairs of plastic
under the wooden floors.

Dreaming on a train from New York
to Philly, you hand out six
notes which become an anthem

to our memories of you:
oak, birch, maple,
apple, cocoa, rubber.
For this reason Martin is dead;
for this reason Malcolm is dead;
for this reason Coltrane is dead;
in the eyes of my first son are the browns
of these men and their music.

REUBEN, REUBEN

I reach from pain
to music great enough
to bring me back,
swollenhead, madness,
lovefruit, a pickle of hate
so sour my mouth twicked
up and would not sing;
there's nothing in the beat
to hold it in
melody and turn human skin;
a brown berry gone
to rot just two days on the branch;
we've lost a son,
the music, *jazz*, comes in.

COLTRANE, SYEEDA'S SONG FLUTE
For M & P. R.

> *When I came across it on the*
> *piano it reminded me of her,*
> *because it sounded like a*
> *happy, child's song.*
>
> COLTRANE

　　　　To Marilyn, to Peter,
playing, making things: the walls, the stairs,
the attics, bright nests in nests;
the slow, light, grave unstitching of lies,
opening, stinking, letting in air

you bear yourselves in, become your own mother
　　　and father,
your own child.
You lying closer.

You going along. Days.
The strobe-lit wheel stops dead
once, twice in a life: old-fashioned rays:

and then all the rest of the time pulls blur,
only you remember it more, playing.

Listening here in the late quiet you can think
great things of us all, I think we will all, Coltrane,
meet speechless and easy in Heaven, our names
known and forgotten, all dearest, all come
    giant-stepping
out into some wide, light, merciful mind.

John
Coltrane, 40, gone
right through the floorboards,
up to the shins, up to the eyes,
closed over,

Syeeda's happy, child's song
left up here, playing.

AFTER THE WAR; WHEN COLTRANE
ONLY WANTED TO PLAY DANCE TUNES
for Larry Levis

The sadness of afternoons was unmistakable.
There was no new way
Of seeing. The woman who left me
Could have returned at any time
Breathless, a strand of dark hair
Caught in the corner
Of her mouth. The dance hall of the Audubon
Still held

Its own particular style
Of forgiveness, as familiar
As the headlines of the old newspapers
Stuffed in the glory holes
Between the stalls of the downstairs toilet.

People kept their distance.
Couples two-stepped in tight circles
Among the pigeons and the dusk
And the dice games of the park.

The boys in the shadows
Were not praying,
But only tying their shoes,
And I moved in my own time,
And listened again for saxophones.

I'm quitting this place soon

Was still the tune
The girls mouthed to the gypsy
Cabs along the avenue.

ALABAMA, *c.* 1963:
A BALLAD BY JOHN COLTRANE

But
Shouldn't this state have a song?
Long, gliding figures of my breath
Of breath
Lost?

Somebody can't sing
Because somebody's gone.
Somebody can't sing
Because somebody's gone.

Shouldn't this landscape
Hold a true anthem?

    What
You can't do?
    Whom
You can't invent?
    Where
You can't stay?
    Why
You won't keep it?

But
Shouldn't this state
Have a song?

And shall we call it
My face will murder me?
And shall we call it

I'm not waiting?

WILLIAM CARLOS WILLIAMS

Didn't like jazz, he once claimed
In an interview,
The good doctor's reaction to it
A bit like a hand retracting
From a slim volume

Of 20th century verse. In
Other words: good intentions,
But what does this *yak, yak, yak*

Have to do with me? This,
You understand, from a person
Who had listened
To an industrial river, forced
A painter's brush to give up
Its low, animal noise,

Broke trees into
Sense.

PHOTO OF JOHN COLTRANE, 1963

Otherworldly and outreaching,
Λ Parnassus of noise with a serious
Glint of inestimable
Worry on his face,

O Coltrane what will ring
From your pious
Gleaming Antillean Euphonia, so capable,
Swift, with no trace,

No trace of stillness? The blur
Of the gray-gray and *gris-gris*
Flows hornward to the black bell

Of the saxophone, a cylinder
Of joy, an empurpled sea
Of heaven ebbing into hell.

FALL DOWN
in memory of eric dolphy

All men are locked in their cells.
Though we quake
In fist of body
Keys rattle, set us free.

I remember and wonder why?
In fall, in summer; times
Will be no more. Journeys
End.
I remember and wonder why?

In the sacred labor of lung
Spine and groin,
You cease, fly away

To what? To autumn, to
Winter, to brown leaves, to
Wind where no lark sings; yet
Through dominion of air, jaw and fire

I remember!

Eric Dolphy, you swung
A beautiful axe. You lived a clean
Life.
You were young—
You died.

FOR ERIC DOLPHY

    on flute
    spinning   spinning   spinning
    love
    thru / out
    the universe

i
know
exactly
whut chew mean
man

you like
tittee
my sister
who never expressed LOVE
in words (like the white folks always   d
she would sit in the corner   o
and cry   i
everytime   n
I   g
got a whuppin

DON'T CRY, SCREAM

for John Coltrane/ from a black poet/
in a basement apt. crying dry tears
of "you ain't gone.")

> into the sixties
> a trane
> came/ out of the
> fifties with a
> golden boxcar
> riding the rails
> of novation.
>> blowing
>> a-melodics
>> screeching,
>> screaming,
>> blasting—
>>> driving some away,
>>> (those paper readers who thought
>>> manhood was something innate)
>>>
>>> bring others in,
>>> (the few who didn't believe that the
>>> world existed around established whi
>>> teness & leonard bernstein)

music that ached.
murdered our minds (we reborn)
born into a neoteric aberration.
& suddenly
you envy the
BLIND man—
you know that he will
hear what you'll never
see.

      your music is like
      my head—nappy black/
      a good nasty feel with
      tangled songs of:
          we-eeeeeeeeeee   sing
          WE-EEEeeeeeeeeee   loud &
          WE-EEEEEEEEEEEEEEEEE high
                                              with
                                              feeling

a people playing
the sound of me when
i combed it. combed at
it.

i cried for billie holiday.
the blues. we ain't blue
the blues exhibited illusions of manhood.
destroyed by you. Ascension into:

    scream-eeeeeeeeeeeeee-ing   sing
    SCREAM-EEEeeeeeeeeeee-ing   loud &
    SCREAM-EEEEEEEEEEEEEE-ing   long with
                                       feeling

we ain't blue, we are black.
we ain't blue, we are black.
                    (all the blues did was
                    make me cry)
soultrane gone on a trip
he left man images
he was a life-style of
man-makers & annihilator
of attache case carriers.

Trane done went.
(got his hat & left me one)
saw brother,
i didn't cry,
i just—
    Scream-eeeeeeeeeeeeeee-ed   sing loud
    SCREAM-EEEEEEEEEEEEEEEEEEEE-ED   & high with
    we-eeeeeeeeeeeeeeeeeeeeeeee ee   feeling

```
WE-EEEEEEeeeeeeeeeEEEEEEEE          letting
WE-EEEEEEEEEEEEEEEEEEEEEEEE          yr/voice
WHERE YOU DONE GONE, BROTHER?        break
```

it hurts, grown babies
dying. born. done caught me
a trane. steel wheels broken
by popsicle sticks. i went out
& tried to buy a nickle bag
wish my standard oil card.

> (swung on a faggot who politely
> scratched his ass in my presence.
> he smiled broken teeth stained from
> his over-used tongue. fisted-face.
> teeth dropped in tune with ray
> charles singing "yesterday.")

blonds had more fun—
with snagga-tooth niggers
who saved pennies & pop bottles for weekends
to play negro & other filthy inventions.
be-bop-en to james brown's
cold sweat—these niggers didn't sweat,
they perspired. & the blond's dye came out,
i ran. she did too, with his pennies, pop bottles
& his mind. tune in next week same time same station
for anti-self in one lesson.

to the negro cow-sissies
who did tchaikovsky &
the beatles & live in
split-level homes & had
split level minds & babies.
who committed the act of
love with their clothes on.

       (who hid in the bathroom to read
       jet mag., who didn't read the chicago
       defender because of the misspelled
       words & had shelves of books by
       europeans on display. untouched. who
       hid their little richard & lightnin'
       slim records & asked: "John who?"

       instant hate.)
they didn't know any better,
brother, they were too busy getting
into debt, expressing humanity &
taking off color.

```
SCREAMMMM/we-eeeee/screech/teee      improvise
aheeeeeeeee/screeeeeee/theeee/ee     with
ahHHHHHHHHH/WEEEEEEEE/scrEEE         feeling
    EEEE
we-eeeeeeWE-EEEEEEEEWE-EE-EEEEE
```

the ofays heard you &
were wiped out. spaced.
one clown asked me during,
my favorite things, if
you were practicing.
i fired on the muthafucka & said,
"i'm practicing."

naw brother,
i didn't cry.
got high off my thoughts—
they kept coming back,
back to destroy me.
& that BLIND man
i don't envy him anymore
i can see his hear
& hear his heard through my pores.
i can see my me. it was truth you gave,
like a daily shit
it had to come.

        can you scream—brother?   very
        can you scream—brother?   soft
i hear you.
i hear you.

and the Gods will too.

HAKI MADHUBUTI (DON LEE)   161

AM/TRAK

Trane,
Trane,
History Love Scream Oh
Trane, Oh
Trane, Oh
Scream History Love
Trane

Begin on by a Philly night club
or the basement of a cullut chuhch
walk the bars my man for pay
honk the night lust of money
oh
blow—
scream history love

Rabbit, Cleanhead, Diz
Big Maybelle, Trees in the shining night forest
Oh
blow
love, history

Alcohol we submit to thee
3x's consume our lives
our livers quiver under yr poison hits
eyes roll back in stupidness

The navy, the lord, niggers,
the streets
all converge a shitty symphony
of screams
   to come
   dazzled invective
Honk Honk Honk, "I am here
to love
it". Let me be fire-mystery
air feeder beauty"
Honk
Oh
scream—Miles
comes.

3

Hip band alright
sum up life in the slick
street part of the
world, oh,
blow,

If you cd
nigger
man

Miles wd stand back and negative check
oh, he dug him—Trane
But Trane clawed at the limits of cool
slandered sanity
with his tryin to be born
raging
shit
    Oh
    blow,
        yeh go do it
        honk, scream
        uhuh yeh—history
                love
                blue clipped moments
                of intense feeling.
"Trane you blows too long".
Screaming niggers drop out yr solos
Bohemian nights, the "heavyweight champ"
smacked him
  in the face
his eyes sagged like a spent
dick, hot vowels escaped the metal clone of his soul
fucking saxophone
tell us shit tell us tell us!

There was nothing left to do but
be where monk cd find him
that crazy
mother fucker

>   duh duh-duh duh-duh duh
>   duh duh
>   duh duh-duh duh-duh duh
>   duh duh
>   duh duh-duh duh-duh duh
>   duh duh
>   duh Duuuuuuuuuhhhhhh

Can you play this shit? (Life asks
Come by and listen

& at the 5 Spot Bach, Mulatto ass Beethoven
& even Duke, who has given America its hip tongue
checked
checked
Trane stood and dug
Crazy monk's shit
Street gospel intellectual mystical survival codes
Intellectual street gospel funk modes
Tink a ling put downs of dumb shit
pink pink a cool bam groove note air breath
a why I'm here
a why I aint

& who is you - ha - you - ha - you - ha
Monk's shit
Blue Cooper 5 Spot
was the world busting
on piano bass drums & tenor

This was Coltrane's College. A Ph motherfuckin d
sitting at the feet, elbows
& funny grin
Of Master T Sphere
   too cool to be a genius
he was instead
Theolonius
with Comrades Shadow
on tubs, lyric Wilbur
who hipped us to electric futures
& the monster with the horn.

5

From the endless sessions
money lord hovers oer us
capitalism beats our ass
dope & juice wont change it
Trane, blow, oh scream
yeh, anyway.

There then came down in the ugly streets of us
inside the head & tongue

of us
a man
black blower of the now
The vectors from all sources—slavery, renaissance
bop charlie parker,
nigger absolute super-sane screams against reality
course through him
AS SOUND!
"Yes, it says
this is now in you screaming
recognize the truth
recognize reality
& even check me (Trane)
who blows it
Yes it says
Yes &
Yes again   Convulsive multi orgasmic
           Art
           Protest

& finally, brother, you took you were
   (are we gathered to dig this?
   electric wind find us finally
   on red records of the history of ourselves)

The cadre came together
the inimitable 4 who blew the pulse of then, exact
The flame the confusion the love of

whatever the fuck there was
    to love
Yes it says
blow, oh honk-scream (bahhhhhhh—wheeeeeeee)

(If Don Lee thinks I am imitating him in this poem,
this is only payback for his imitating me—we
are brothers, even if he is a backward cultural
    nationalist
motherfucker—Hey man only socialism brought by
    revolution
can win)

           Trane was the spirit of the 60's
           He was Malcolm X in New Super Bop Fire
           Baaahhhhh
           Wheeeeee . . . . Black Art!!!
Love
History
   On The Bar Tops of Philly
in the Monkish College of *Express*
in the cool Grottoes of Miles Davis Funnytimery
Be
Be
Be reality
Be reality alive in motion in flame to change
    (You Knew It!)
                        to change!!

                    (All you reactionaries listening
                    Fuck you, Kill you
                    get outta here!!!)

Jimmy Garrison, bass, McCoy Tyner, piano, Captain
     Marvel Elvin
on drums, the number itself—the precise saying
all of it in it afire aflame talking saying being doing
     meaning
Meditations,
Expressions
A Love Supreme
(I lay in solitary confinement, July 67
     Tanks rolling thru Newark
     & whistled all I knew of Trane
     my knowledge heartbeat
     & he was *dead*
they
said.
And yet last night I played *Meditations*
& it told me what to do
Live, you crazy mother
fucker!
     Live!
     & organize
     yr shit
     as rightly
     burning!

AMIRI BARAKA (LEROI JONES)   169

TRANE

Propped against the crowded bar
he pours into the curved and silver horn
his old unhappy longing for a home

the dancers twist and turn
he leans and wishes he could burn
his memories to ashes like some old notorious emperor

of rome. but no stars blazed across the sky when he
        was born
no wise men found his hovel; this crowded bar
where dancers twist and turn,

holds all the fame and recognition he will ever earn
on earth or heaven. he leans against the bar
and pours his old unhappy longing in the saxophone

BLUES FOR JOHN COLTRANE,
DEAD AT 41

Although my house floats on a lawn
as plush as a starlet's body
and my sons sleep easily,
I think of death's salmon breath
leaping back up the saxophone
with its wet kiss.

Hearing him dead,
I feel it in my feet
as if the house were rocked
by waves from a soundless speedboat
planing by, full throttle.

WILLIAM MATTHEWS   171

SOLOING

My mother tells me she dreamed
of John Coltrane, a young Trane
playing his music with such joy
and contained energy and rage
she could not hold back her tears.
And sitting awake now, her hands
crossed in her lap, the tears start
in her blind eyes. The TV set
behind her is gray, expressionless.
It is late, the neighbors quiet,
even the city—Los Angeles—quiet.
I have driven for hours down 99,
over the Grapevine into heaven
to be here. I place my left hand
on her shoulder, and she smiles.
What a world, a mother and son
finding solace in California
just where we were told it would
be, among the palm trees and all-
night super markets pushing orange
back-lighted oranges at 2 A.M.
"He was alone," she says, and does
not say, just as I am, "soloing."
What a world, a great man half
her age comes to my mother

in sleep to give her the gift
of song, which—shaking the tears
away—she passes on to me, for now
I can hear the music of the world
in the silence and that word:
soloing. What a world—when I
arrived the great bowl of mountains
was hidden in a cloud of exhaust,
the sea spread out like a carpet
of oil, the roses I had brought
from Fresno browned on the seat
beside me, and I could have
turned back and lost the music.

"JOHN COLTRANE ARRIVED
WITH AN EGYPTIAN LADY"
—belated prayer—

no sheet of sound enshroud
the Fount of this fevered
    Brook becoming one
with God's Eye, not
   a one of these notes

come near to the brunt
   of the inaudible
note I've been reach-
   ing towards

            To whatever
    dust-eyed giver
of tone to whatever
talk, to whatever slack
   jaws drawn against bone

            To whatever
   hearts abulge with
unsourced light, to whatever
   sun, to whatever moist
inward meats
              of love

Tonight I'll bask
beneath an arch of
                lost
voices,   echo
    some Other place,
Nut's nether suns
                These
notes' long fingers gathered
    come to grips of gathered
cloud, connected lip
                to unheard of

    tongue

RHYTHM SECTION

The rhythm of life
Is a jazz rhythm,
Honey.
The gods are laughing at us.

LANGSTON HUGHES
Lenox Avenue: Midnight

JAZZ

I'd like to know everything
A jazz artist knows, starting with the song
"Goodbye Pork Pie Hat."

Like to make some songs myself:
"Goodbye Rickshaw,"
"Goodbye Lemondrop,"
"Goodbye Rendezvous."

Or maybe even blues:

If you fall in love with me I'll make you pancakes
All morning. If you fall in love with me
I'll make you pancakes all night.
If you don't like pancakes
We'll go to the creperie. If you don't like pancakes
We'll go to the creperie.
If you don't like to eat, handsome boy,
Don't you hang around with me.

On second thought, I'd rather find
The fanciest music I can, and hear all of it.

I'd rather love somebody
And say his name to myself every day
Until I fall apart.

ANGELA BALL   179

MINGUS AT THE SHOWPLACE

I was miserable, of course, for I was seventeen,
and so I swung into action and wrote a poem,

and it was miserable, for that was how I thought
poetry worked: you digested experience and shat

literature. It was 1960 at The Showplace, long since
defunct, on West 4th St., and I sat at the bar,

casting beer money from a thin reel of ones,
the kid in the city, big ears like a puppy.

And I knew Mingus was a genius. I knew two
other things but as it happened they were wrong.

So I made him look at the poem.
"There's a lot of that going around," he said,

and Sweet Baby Jesus he was right. He glowered
at me but he didn't look as if he thought

bad poems were dangerous, the way some poets do.
If they were baseball executives they'd plot

to destroy sandlots everywhere so that the game
could be saved from children. Of course later

that night he fired his pianist in mid-number
and flurried him from the stand.

"We've suffered a diminuendo in personnel,"
he explained, and the band played on.

BUD POWELL, PARIS, 1959

I'd never seen pain so bland.
Smack, though I didn't call it smack
in 1959, had eaten his technique.
His white-water right hand clattered
missing runs nobody else would think
to try, nor think to be outsmarted
by. Nobody played as well
as Powell, and neither did he,
stalled on his bench between sets,
stolid and vague, my hero,
his mocha skin souring gray.
Two bucks for a Scotch in this dump,
I thought, and I bought me
another. I was young and pain
rose to my ceiling, like warmth,
like a story that makes us come true
in the present. Each day's
melodrama in Powell's cells
bored and lulled him. Pain loves pain
and calls it company, and it is.

ONE O'CLOCK JUMP

Still tingling with Basie's hard cooking,
between sets I stood at the bar
when the man next to me ordered
scotch and milk. I looked to see who had
this stray taste and almost swooned
when I saw it was the master.
Basie knocked his shot back,
then, when he saw me gaping,
raised his milk to my peachy face
and rolled out his complete smile
before going off with friends
to leave me in that state of grace.

A year later I was renting rooms
from a woman named Tillie who wanted
no jazz in her dank, unhallowed house.
Objecting even to lowest volume of solo piano,
she'd puff upstairs to bang on my door.

I grew opaque, unwell,
slouched to other apartments,
begging to play records.
Duked, dePrezed, and unBased,
longing for Billy, Monk, Brute, or Zoot,
I lived in silence through
that whole lost summer.

Still, aware of divine favor, I bided time
and waited for the day of reckoning.
My last night in Tillie's godless house,
late—when I knew she was hard asleep—
I gave her the full One O'Clock Jump,
having Basie ride his horse of perfect time
like an avenging angel over top volume,
hoisting his scotch and milk as he galloped
into Tillie's ear, headlong down her throat
to roar all night in her sulphurous organs.

FOR ART BLAKEY AND
THE JAZZ MESSENGERS

For the sound we revere
we dub you art as continuum
as spirit as sound of depth
here to stay

        In my young years
I heard you bopping and weaving
messages I could only walk to
where wood mates with skin

I would have dubbed you godhead
but your sound rolled and pealed:
I am the drumhead even though
Blue Note don't care nothing
bout nothing but profit

How you sound is
who you are
where your ear
leans moaning or bopping
from the amen corner
of chicken and dumpling
memories and places

In my young years
I would have dubbed you
something strange as god
of opiate heaven
of brutal contact
of bible and rifle memories

But the drumhead rolled my name:
How you sound is
who you are
like drumsound
backing back to root
roosting at the meeting place
the time that has always been here

Even here where wood
mates with skin on wax
to make memory, to place us
even in this hideous place
pp-ppounding pp-ppounding
the ss-sssounds of who
we are even in this place
of strange and brutal design

SHAKING HANDS WITH MONGO
for Mongo Santamaría

Mongo's open hands:
huge soft palms
that drop the hard seeds
of conga with a thump,
shaken by the god of hurricanes,
raining mambo coconuts
that do not split
even when they hit the sidewalk,
rumbling incantation
in the astonished dancehall
of a city in winter,
sweating in a rush of A-train night,
so that Chano Pozo,
maestro of the drumming Yoruba heart,
howling Manteca in a distant coro,
hears Mongo and yes,
begins to bop
a slow knocking bolero of forgiveness
to the nameless man
who shot his life away
for a bag of tecata
in a Harlem bar
forty years ago

MARTÍN ESPADA   187

COPACETIC MINGUS

"Mingus One, Two and Three.
Which is the image you want the world to see?"
CHARLES MINGUS, *Beneath the Underdog*

Heartstring. Blessed wood
& every moment the thing's made of:
ball of fatback
licked by fingers of fire.
Hard love, it's hard love.
Running big hands down
the upright's wide hips,
rocking his moon-eyed mistress
with gold in her teeth.
Art & life bleed
into each other
as he works the bow.
But tonight we're both a long ways
from the Mile High City,
1973. Here in New Orleans
years below sea level,
I listen to *Pithecanthropus
Erectus*: Up & down, under
& over, every which way—
thump, thump, dada—ah, yes.
Wood heavy with tenderness,

Mingus fingers the loom
gone on Segovia,
dogging the raw strings
unwaxed with rosin.
Hyperbolic bass line. Oh, no!
Hard love, it's hard love.

ELEGY FOR THELONIOUS

Damn the snow.
Its senseless beauty
pours a hard light
through the hemlock.
Thelonious is dead. Winter
drifts in the hourglass;
notes pour from the brain cup.
Damn the alley cat
wailing a muted dirge
off Lenox Ave.
Thelonious is dead.
Tonight's a lazy rhapsody of shadows
swaying to blue vertigo
& metaphysical funk.
Black trees in the wind.
Crepuscule with Nelly
plays inside the bowed head.
"Dig the Man Ray of piano!"
O Satisfaction,
hot fingers blur
on those white rib keys.
Coming on the Hudson.
Monk's Dream.
The ghost of bebop
from 52nd Street,

footprints in the snow.
Damn February.
Let's go to Minton's
& play "modern malice"
till daybreak. Lord,
there's Thelonious
wearing that old funky hat
pulled down over his eyes.

CREPUSCULE WITH NELLIE
For Ira

Monk at the Five Spot
  late one night.
Ruby my Dear, Epistrophy.
  The place nearly empty
Because of the cold spell.
One beautiful black transvestite
  alone up front,
Sipping his drink demurely.

The music Pythagorean,
  one note at a time
Connecting the heavenly spheres,
While I leaned against the bar
  surveying the premises
Through cigarette smoke.

All of a sudden, a clear sense
  of a memorable occasion...
The joy of it, the delicious melancholy...
This very strange man bent over the piano
  shaking his head, humming...

Misterioso.

Then it was all over, thank you!
Chairs being stacked up on tables,
    their legs up.
The prospect of the freeze outside,
    the long walk home,
Making one procrastinatory.

Who said Americans don't have history,
    only endless nostalgia?
And where the hell was Nellie?

SNOW

I cannot help noticing how this slow Monk solo
seems to go somehow
with the snow
that is coming down this morning,

how the notes and the spaces accompany
its easy falling
on the geometry of the ground,
on the flagstone path,
the slanted roof,
and the angles of the split rail fence

as if he had imagined a winter scene
as he sat at the piano
late one night at the Five Spot
playing "Ruby My Dear."

Then again, it's the kind of song
that would go easily with rain
or a tumult of leaves,

and for that matter it's a snow
that could attend
an adagio for strings,
the best of the Ronettes,
or George Thorogood and the Destroyers.

It falls so indifferently
into the spacious white parlor of the world,
if I were sitting here reading
in silence,
reading the morning paper
or reading *Being and Nothingness,*
not even letting the spoon
touch the inside of the cup,
I have a feeling
the snow would even go perfectly with that.

THELONIOUS SPHERE MONK

Cold, the day you leave
you can use that hat.
Ahh Monk, the station fades
as the suburbs begin
you bent the notes right
they will not lose their ring.
I see your shuffle dance
up from the 5 Spot piano
and hear you, wordless, sing.

LISTENING IMAGES

LESTER YOUNG

Yes, clouds do have
The smoothest sound.

BILLIE HOLIDAY

Hold a microphone
Close to the moon.

COLEMAN HAWKINS

A hawk for certain,
But as big as a man.

BEN WEBSTER

Such fragile moss
In a massive tree.

LOUIS ARMSTRONG

Just dip your ears
And taste the sauce.

ROY ELDRIDGE

Get in the car.
Start the engine.

DIZZY GILLESPIE

Gusts of gusto
Sweep the desert.

CLIFFORD BROWN

A fine congregation
This spring morning.

ART TATUM

Innumerable dew,
A splendid web.

BUD POWELL

The eye, and then
The hurricane.

THELONIOUS MONK

Always old, always new,
Always déjà vu.

COUNT BASIE

Acorns on the roof—
Syncopated oakestra.

JOHN COLTRANE

Sunrise golden
At the throat.

ERIC DOLPHY

Coming across quick
Deer in the forest.

DELTA BLUES

They broke bottles
Just to get the neck.

SON HOUSE

A lone man plucking
Bolts of lightning.

KANSAS CITY SHOUTERS

Your baby leaves you on the train.
You stand and bring it back again.

BIG JOE TURNER

Big as laughter, big as rain,
Big as the big public domain.

RUBY MY DEAR
Thelonious Monk, 1959

You are back again, re-entering the central train of trails: the quintessential U.S.A. of drowsy fields and sleepy fastfood chains; the U.S.A. of nipped buds and layaways negotiated in harsh, flatland cracker accents. Surrounded by them, hemmed in, you sometimes feel a little like one of those brainy slicksters over at the Federal Penitentiary in Milan, Michigan, for, like them, you're locked up and keyed down.

"Ruby My Dear" comes drifting down Lake Huron in the saline marshlands of an eternal summer. The midwestern night is steamy hot with mosquitoes, the air knotted and thick with gnats like Monk's gracefully gnarled chordal clusters; notes and spiraling nodes, encoded, glistening like Milky Way-encrusted swirls and specks of darkness.

You know what you're hearing is human yearning, and rushes of the Divine calling you home to all the Africanized galaxies in this shimmering island universe.

FREE JAZZ

DARK TO THEMSELVES

Invent, experiment—Jazz
that doesn't swing but dances tight

as a drumhead so taut it might
explode: whole notes cleaved

into sixteenths with a single blow, melodies
recoded as arpeggios. *Say, what he call this*

composition? Tiny fingers divining
an architectonic flow, forearms jacking

cracks in the keyboard as wire
and wood cry out in agony:

duo follow, ringing changes.
Liberate the dissonance without killing

the blues. Unit structure: cut it.
They don't teach this joint in the Conservatory.

Varèse via Jelly Roll, serial Waller,
harmony ribbons in a Möbius strip. Recut it.

Enough is enough. Brother can't play
here again, the customers ain't paying.

Even Miles was giggling in the darkness.
It's always a bitch to be out

front. He summons the bassline
of his thoughts in the shadows, tracing a new theory

of silence. Don't worry about the next gig.
Their ears are still learning.

LEAVING SATURN
Sun Ra & His Year 2000 Myth Science
Arkestra at Grendel's Lair Cabaret, 1986

Skyrocketed—
My eyes dilate old
Copper pennies.
Effortlessly, I play
*
Manifesto of the One
Stringed Harp. Only
This time I'm washed
Ashore, shipwrecked
*
In Birmingham.
My black porcelain
Fingers, my sole
Possession. So I
*
Hammer out
Equations for
A New Thing.
Ogommetelli,
*
Ovid & Homer
Behind me, I toss
Apple peelings in
The air & half-hear

*
Brush strokes, the up
Kick of autumn
Leaves, the Arkestra
Laying down for
*
New dimensions.
I could be at Berkeley
Teaching a course—
Fixin's: How to Dress
*
Myth or Generations:
Spaceships in Harlem.
Instead, vibes from Chi-
Town, must be Fletcher's
*
Big Band Music—oh,
My brother, the wind—
I know this life is
Only a circus. I'm
*
Brushed aside: a naïf,
A charlatan, too avant-
Garde. Satellite music for
A futuristic tent, says

*

One critic. Heartbreak
In outer space, says
Another,—lunar
Dust on the brain.

*

I head to New York.
New York loves
A spectacle: wet pain
Of cement, sweet

*

Scent of gulls swirling
Between skyscrapers
So tall, looks like war.
If what I'm told is true,

*

Mars is dying, it's after
The end of the world.
So, here I am,
In Philadelphia,

*

Death's headquarters,
Here to save the cosmos,
Here to dance in a bed
Of living gravestones.

MAJOR JACKSON   209

C.T.'S VARIATION

some springs the mississippi rose up so high
it drowned the sound of singing and escape
that sound of jazz from back
boarded shanties by railroad tracks
visionary women letting pigeons loose
on unsettled skies
was drowned by the quiet ballad of natural disaster
some springs song was sweeter even so
sudden cracks split the sky / for only a second
lighting us in a kind of laughter
as we rolled around quilted histories
extended our arms and cries to the rain
that kept us soft together

some springs the mississippi rose up so high
it drowned the sound of singing and escape
church sisters prayed and rinsed
the brown dinge tinting linens
thanked the trees for breeze
and the greenness sticking to the windows
the sound of jazz from back
boarded shanties by railroad tracks
visionary women letting pigeons loose
on unsettled skies
some springs song was sweeter even so

From WRITTEN TO MUSIC

if the pain is greater
than the difference
as the bird in the night
or the perfumes in the moon
oh witch of question
oh lips of submission
in the flesh of summer
the silver slipper
in the sleeping forest
if hope surpasses the question
by the mossy spring
in the noon of harvest
between the pillars of silk
in the luminous difference
oh tongue of music
oh teacher of splendor
if the meat of the heart
if the fluid of the wing
as love
if birth
or trust as
love as love

*

time turns like tables
the indifferent and blissful Spring
saves all souls and seeds and slaves asleep
dark Spring
in the dark whispering human will
words spoken by two kissing tongues
hissing union
Eve's snake
stars come on
two naked bodies tumble
through bodiless Christmas trees
blazing like bees and rosebuds
fire turns to falling powder
lips relax and smile and sleep
fire sweeps
the hearth of the blood
on far off red double stars
they probate their own tied wills

MUSIC FOR HOMEMADE INSTRUMENTS
improvising with Douglas Ewart

I dug you artless, I dug you out. Did you re-do? You
dug me less, art. You dug, let's do art. You dug me, less
art. Did you re-do? If I left art out, you dug. My artless
dug-out. You dug, let art out. Did you re-do, dug-out
canoe? Easy as a porkpie piper-led cinch. Easy as a baby
bounce. Hop on pot, tin pan man. Original abstract, did
you re-do it? Betting on shy cargo, strutting dimpled
low-cal strumpets employ a hipster to blow up the
native formica. Then divide efficiency on hairnets,
flukes, faux saxons. You dug me out, didn't you? Did
you re-do? Ever curtained to experiment with strumpet
strutting. Now curtains to milk laboratory. Desecrated
flukes & panics displayed by mute politicians all over
this whirly-gig. Hey, you dug! Art lasts. Did you re-do?
Well-known mocker of lurching unused brains, tribal
& lustrous diddlysquats, Latin dimension crepe paper &
muscular stacks. Curtains for perky strumpets strutting
with mites in the twilight of their origami funkier
purses. Artless, you dug. Did you re-do? For patting
wood at flatland, thanks. For bamboozle flukes at Bama,
my seedy medication. Thanks for my name in the
yoohoo. Continental camp-out, percolating throughout
the whirly-gig on faux saxon flukes. You dug art, didn't
you? Did you re-do?

GYRE'S GALAX

Sound variegated through beneath lit
Sound variegated through beneath lit
through sound beneath variegated lit
sound variegated through beneath lit

Variegated sound through beneath lit dark
Variegated sound through beneath lit dark
sound variegated through beneath lit
variegated sound through beneath lit dark

Through variegated beneath sound lit
Through variegated beneath sound lit
through variegated beneath sound lit
through variegated beneath sound lit
Through variegated beneath sound lit
Through variegated beneath sound lit
through beneath lit
through beneath lit
through beneath lit
through beneath lit
Thru beneath
Thru beneath
Thru beneath
through beneath lit
Thru beneath

through beneath lit
Thru beneath
through beneath lit
Thru beneath
Thru beneath
through beneath lit
Thru beneath
Thru beneath
through beneath lit
Thru beneath
Thru beneath
Thru beneath
Thru beneath
Thru beneath
Thru beneath
Thru beneath
Through beneath lit

Twainly ample of amongst
twainly ample of amongst
Twainly ample of amongst
twainly ample of amongst
Twainly ample of amongst
twainly ample of amongst
In lit black viewly

viewly
viewly
in viewly
viewly
viewly
in viewly
viewly
in viewly
viewly
in viewly
viewly
viewly
viewly
in viewly
viewly
In lit black viewly
in dark to stark
In dark to stark
In dark to stark
in dark to stark
In dark to stark
in dark to stark
In dark to stark lit
In above beneath
In above beneath
In above beneath
above beneath lit

above beneath
above beneath
above beneath
above beneath lit
above beneath
above beneath lit
above beneath
above beneath lit
above beneath
above beneath
above beneath
above beneath
above beneath lit
above beneath
above beneath
above beneath lit
above beneath
above beneath
above beneath
above beneath
above beneath
above beneath
above beneath
above beneath
above beneath lit

EPISTROPHE

It's such a static reference; looking
out the window all the time! the eyes' limits...
On good days, the sun.

& what you see. (here in New York)
Walls and buildings; or in the hidden gardens
of opulent Queens: profusion, endless stretches
    of leisure.

It's like being chained to some dead actress:
& she keeps trying to tell you something horribly
    maudlin.

e.g. ("the leaves are flat & motionless.")

What I know of the mind
seems to end here;
Just outside my face.

I wish some weird looking animal
would come along.

MUTING

for Billie Holiday

BILLIE HOLIDAY

Here lies a lady. Day was her double pain,
Pride and compassion equally gone wrong.
At night she sang, "Do you conceive my song?"
And answered in her torn voice, "Don't explain."

HAYDEN CARRUTH

SONG FOR BILLIE HOLIDAY

What can purge my heart
    Of the song
    And the sadness?
What can purge my heart
    But the song
    Of the sadness?
What can purge my heart
    Of the sadness
    Of the song?

Do not speak of sorrow
With dust in her hair,
Or bits of dust in eyes
A chance wind blows there.
The sorrow that I speak of
Is dusted with despair.

Voice of muted trumpet,
Cold brass in warm air.
Bitter television blurred
By sound that shimmers—
    Where?

STRANGE FRUIT

Southern trees bear a strange fruit,
Blood on the leaves and blood at the root,
Black body swinging in the Southern breeze,
Strange fruit hanging from the poplar trees.
Pastoral scene of the gallant South,
The bulging eyes and the twisted mouth,
Scent of magnolia sweet and fresh,
And the sudden smell of burning flesh!
Here is a fruit for the crows to pluck,
For the rain to gather, for the wind to suck
For the sun to rot, for a tree to drop,
Here is a strange and bitter crop.

GOD BLESS THE CHILD

Them that's got shall get,
Them that's not shall lose,
So the Bible said, and it still is news.
Mama may have,
Papa may have,
But God bless the child that got his own!
That's got his own.

Yes, the strong gets more
While the weak ones fade.
Empty pockets don't ever make the grade.
Mama may have,
Papa may have,
But God bless the child that's got his own!
That's got his own.
Money, you got lots o'friends
Crowdin' round the door.
When you're gone and spendin' ends,
They don't come no more.
Rich relations give, crust of bread and such,
You can help yourself, but don't take too much!
Mama may have,
Papa may have,
But God bless the child that's got his own!
That's got his own.

BILLIE HOLIDAY AND ARTHUR HERZOG, JR.   223

STARDUST

Lady sings
the blues
the reds, whatever

she can find—
short
changed, a chord—

God bless
the child
that's got his own

& won't mind
sharing some—
"BILLIES BOUNCE"

"BILLIES BOUNCE"
Miss Holiday's up
on four counts

of possession, three-
fifths, the law
—locked up—

licked—the salt
the boot—refused
a chance to belt

tunes in the clubs—
ex-con. Man,
she got it

bad—Brother
can you spare
a dime

bag? MEANDERING
WARMING UP
A RIFF—

she's all scat,
waxing—
SIDE A

SIDE B
OOH
SHOO DE

OBEE—
detoxed, thawed
in time

for Thanksgiving—live
as ammo, smoking
—NOV. 26 1945—

Day cold as turkey—

THE SECRET LIFE OF MUSICAL
INSTRUMENTS
For Claudia Burson

Between midnight and Reno
the world borders on a dune.
The bus does not stop.

The boys in the band have their heads on the rest.
They dream like so-and-sos.

The woman smokes
one after another.
She is humming "Strange Fruit."
There is smoke in her clothes, her voice,
but her hair never smells.

She blows white petals off her lapel,
tastes salt.
It is a copacetic moon.

The instruments do not sleep in their dark cribs.
They keep cool, meditate.
They have speech with strangers:

Come all ye faithless
young and crazy victims of love.

Come the lowlife and the highborn
all ye upside-down shitasses.

Bring your own light.
Come in. Be lost. Be still.
If you miss us at home
we'll be on our way to the reckoning.

LADY SINGS THE BLUES

Satin luscious, amber Beauty center-stage;
        gardenia in her hair. If flowers could sing
they'd sound like this. That legendary scene:
        the lady unpetals her song, the only light

in a room of smoke, nightclub tinkering
        with lovers in the dark, cigarette flares,
gin & tonic. This is where the heartache
        blooms. Forget the holes

zippered along her arms. Forget the booze.
        Center-stage, satin-tongue dispels a note.

Amber amaryllis, blue chanteuse, Amen.
        If flowers could sing they'd sound like this.

*   *   *

This should be Harlem, but it's not.
        It's Diana Ross with no *Supremes*.
Fox Theater, Nineteen Seventy-something.
        Ma and me; lovers crowded in the dark.

The only light breaks on the movie-screen.
        I'm a boy, but old enough to know *Heartache*.

We watch her rise and wither
        like a burnt-out cliche. You know the story:

Brutal lush. Jail-bird. Scag queen.
        In the asylum scene, the actress's eyes
are bruised; latticed with blood, but not quite sad
        enough. She's the star so her beauty persists.

Not like Billie: fucked-up satin, hair museless,
        heart ruined by the end.

        *   *   *

The houselights wake and nobody's blue but Ma.
        Billie didn't sound like that, she says
as we walk hand in hand to the street.
        Nineteen Seventy-something,

My lady hums, *Good Morning Heartache,*
        My father's in a distant place.

POEM IN WHICH I MAKE THE MISTAKE OF COMPARING BILLIE HOLIDAY TO A COSMIC WASHERWOMAN

We were driving back from the record store at the mall
when Terrance told me that Billie Holiday
was not a symbol for the black soul.

He said, The night is not African American either, for
        your information,

it is just goddamn dark,
and in the background

she was singing a song I never heard before,
moving her voice like water moving
along the shore of a lake,
reaching gently into the crevices, touching the pebbles
        and sand.

Once through the dirty window of a train
on the outskirts of Hoboken, New Jersey,
I swear I saw a sonnet written high up on a
        concrete wall,

rhymed quatrains rising from the
dyslexic alphabet of gang signs and obscenities,

and Terrance says he saw a fresco
of brown and white angels flying
on a boarded-up building in Chinatown

and everybody knows
there's a teenage genius somewhere out there,
a firebrand out of Ghana by way of Alabama,
this very minute in a warehouse loft,
rewriting *Moby-Dick—The Story of the Great
    Black Whale.*

When he bursts out of the womb
                         of his American youth
with his dictionary and his hip-hop shovel,

when he takes his place on stage,
dripping the amniotic fluid of history,
he won't be any color we ever saw before,

and I know he's right, Terrance is right, it's
    so obvious.

But here in the past of that future,
Billie Holiday is still singing
                    a song so dark and slow
it seems bigger than her, it sounds very heavy

like a terrible stain soaked into the sheets,
so deep that nothing will ever get it out,
but she keeps trying,

she keeps pushing the dark syllables under the water
then pulling them up to see if they are clean
but they never are
and it makes her sad
and we are too

and it's dark around the car and inside also is very
        dark.
Terrance and I can barely see each other
in the dashboard glow.
I can only imagine him right now
pointing at the radio
as if to say, Shut up and listen.

FOR OUR LADY

yeh.
       billie.   if someone
had loved u like u
shud have been loved
ain't no tellen what
kinds of songs
               u wud have swung
gainst this country's wite mind.
or what kinds of lyrics
                     wud have pushed us from
our blue / nites.
         yeh.   billie.
if some blk / man
           had reallee
made u feel
         permanentlee warm.
ain't no tellen
           where the jazz of yo/songs
             wud have led us.

WHAT I'M WILD FOR

I broke when I was ten and forty-
year-old Mr. D. was clambering on top of me
and it was all I could do to kick him back, keep
the red ceiling light in sight, and wait
for her to find me. So this is what she's on
her knees for every night, praying
for Pops to come on back, rip her skirt off
and ride her until it's only skin she ever wants
to feel again. I wanted to fling that in her face
the way a slick trumpeter cat from Philly
flung my panties at me summer I was fifteen.

I've seen more love in Alderson, behind
the warden's back, behind Jim Crow's back
on the way home from movies: dykes would touch
hands, feed cigarettes to one another
like they were kisses, before the cells broke us all up—
forgers, whores, boosters, pushers, users.

The soldiers had it, too, begging for pieces
of my dress and stockings, tearing them to petals
under their noses because *they have the smell
of woman on them*. I could love a whole
army like that. But two husbands later

and the hungry I feel is not the 600-miles-a-night
on a bus flashing slow silver between gigs
while my stomach opens wide. The cure
for that is simple as a couple bucks, red beans
and rice. What I'm wild for is a few grains
of dope and the shakes I get from head to satin
feet when it's "Strange Fruit." One night, my
    body can't
hold me down, the notes break clean, and no one
can see me, but they point to the voice flying over
the band and say, *Billie, nobody sings
hunger like you do, or love.*

THE DAY LADY DIED

It is 12:20 in New York a Friday
three days after Bastille Day, yes
it is 1959 and I go get a shoeshine
because I will get off the 4:19 in Easthampton
at 7:15 and then go straight to dinner
and I don't know the people who will feed me

I walk up the muggy street beginning to sun
and have a hamburger and a malted and buy
an ugly NEW WORLD WRITING to see what the poets
in Ghana are doing these days
                         I go on to the bank
and Miss Stillwagon (first name Linda I once heard)
doesn't even look up my balance for once in her life
and in the GOLDEN GRIFFIN I get a little Verlaine
for Patsy with drawings by Bonnard although I do
think of Hesiod, trans. Richmond Lattimore or
Brendan Behan's new play or *Le Balcon* or *Les Nègres*
of Genet, but I don't, I stick with Verlaine
after practically going to sleep with quandariness

and for Mike I just stroll into the PARK LANE
Liquor Store and ask for a bottle of Strega and
then I go back where I came from to 6th Avenue
and the tobacconist in the Ziegfeld Theatre and
casually ask for a carton of Gauloises and a carton
of Picayunes, and a NEW YORK POST with her face on it

and I am sweating a lot by now and thinking of
leaning on the john door in the FIVE SPOT
while she whispered a song along the keyboard
to Mal Waldron and everyone and I stopped breathing

CANARY
For Michael S. Harper

Billie Holiday's burned voice
had as many shadows as lights,
a mournful candelabra against a sleek piano,
the gardenia her signature under that ruined face.

(Now you're cooking, drummer to bass,
magic spoon, magic needle.
Take all day if you have to
with your mirror and your bracelet of song.)

Fact is, the invention of women under siege
has been to sharpen love in the service of myth.

If you can't be free, be a mystery.

THE JOURNEY

Miles was waiting on the dock,
his trumpet in a paper bag.

Lady was cold—
wind lashed the gardenias
I stole for her hair.

We were shabby, the three of us.

No one was coming so I started to row.

It was hard going—
stagnant, meandering...

The city moaned and smoldered.
Tin cans on the banks like shackles...

To be discovered, in the open...

But Miles took out his horn
and played.
Lady sang.

A slow traditional blues.

The current caught us—
horn, voice, oar stroking water ...

I don't know how long we floated—

our craft so full of music,
the night so full of stars.

When I awoke we were entering an ocean,
sun low on water
warm as a throat,
gold as a trumpet.

We wept.

Then soared in a spiritual.

Never have I been so happy.

LIST OF AUTHORS

Elizabeth Alexander b. 1962
Lewis Allan 1903–1986
Angela Ball b. 1952
Amiri Baraka (LeRoi Jones) b. 1934
Ted Berrigan 1934–1983
Paul Blackburn 1926–1971
Max Bodenheim 1892–1954
Catherine Bowman b. 1957
Kamau Brathwaite b. 1930
Gwendolyn Brooks 1917–2000
Frank London Brown 1927–1962
Sterling A. Brown 1901–1989
Darrell Burton 1960–2002
Hayden Carruth b. 1921
Janet M. Choi
Billy Collins b. 1941
William Corbett b. 1948
Gregory Corso 1930–2001
Jayne Cortez b. 1936
Robert Creeley 1926–2005
E. E. Cummings 1894–1962
Waring Cuney 1906–1976
Kyle Dargan
Frank Marshall Davis 1905–1987
Thulani Davis b. 1948

Owen Dodson 1914–1983
Mark Doty b. 1953
Rita Dove b. 1952
Cornelius Eady b. 1954
Martín Espada b. 1957
Dana Gioia b. 1950
Matthew Graham
Michael S. Harper b. 1938
Terrance Hayes b. 1971
Calvin Hernton 1933–2001
Arthur Herzog, Jr.
Edward Hirsch b. 1950
Tony Hoagland b. 1953
Billie Holiday 1915–1959
Langston Hughes 1902–1967
Lawson Fusao Inada b. 1938
Major Jackson b. 1968
Ted Joans 1928–2003
Helene Johnson 1905–1995
Patricia Spears Jones b. 1951
Bob Kaufman 1925–1986
John Keene b. 1965
Keorapetse Kgositsile b. 1938
Etheridge Knight 1931–1991
Yusef Komunyakaa b. 1937
Philip Larkin 1922–1985
David Lehman b. 1948

Philip Levine b. 1928
Vachel Lindsay 1879–1931
Nathaniel Mackey b. 1947
Haki Madhubuti (Don Lee) b. 1942
Clarence Major b. 1936
Dionisio D. Martinez b. 1956
William Matthews 1942–1997
Ernst Moerman 1897–1944
Harryette Mullen
Frank O'Hara 1926–1966
Robert Pinsky b. 1940
King Pleasure (Clarence Beeks) 1922–1981
Sterling D. Plumpp b. 1940
N. H. Pritchard
Lucien Quincy b. 1969
Andy Razaf 1895–1973
Kenneth Rexroth 1905–1982
Muriel Rukeyser 1913–1980
Sonia Sanchez b. 1934
Carl Sandburg 1878–1967
Robert Sargent b. 1912
Ntozake Shange b. 1948
Charles Simic b. 1938
Sean Singer b. 1974
A. B. Spellman b. 1935
Billy Strayhorn 1915–1967
Quincy Troupe b. 1943

Jean Valentine b. 1934
William Carlos Williams 1883–1963
C. D. Wright b. 1949
Charles Wright b. 1935
Al Young b. 1939
Kevin Young b. 1970
Paul Zimmer b. 1934

ACKNOWLEDGMENTS

Thanks are due to the following copyright holders for permission to reprint:

ELIZABETH ALEXANDER: "Billy Strayhorn Writes 'Lush Life'" copyright © 2005 by Elizabeth Alexander. Reprinted from *American Sublime* with the permission of Graywolf Press, Saint Paul, Minnesota. "Four Bongos: Take a Train" by Elizabeth Alexander copyright © 1990 by the Rector and Visitors of the University of Virginia. Reprinted from *The Venus Hottentot* with the permission of Graywolf Press, Saint Paul, Minnesota. LEWIS ALLAN: "Strange Fruit" written by Lewis Allan used by permission of Edward B. Marks Music Company. Copyright © 1939 (renewed) by Music Sales Corporation (ASCAP). International copyright secured. All rights reserved. Reprinted by permission. ANGELA BALL: "Jazz" was first published in *The Nebraska Review*. AMIRI BARAKA: "Pres Spoke in a Language" and "Epistrophe" by Amiri Baraka, reprinted by permission of SLL/Sterling Lord Literistic, Inc. Copyright © by Amiri Baraka. "Am/Trak" from *Black Magic Poetry* by Amiri Baraka. Copyright © 1969 by Amiri Baraka. Reprinted by permission of SLL/Sterling Lord Literistic, Inc. TED BERRIGAN: "String of Pearls" from *So Going Around the Cities*, Berkeley Press. Used by permission. PAUL BLACKBURN: "Listening to Sonny Rollins at the Five Spot" from *Selected Poems of Paul Blackburn.* Copyright © 1955, 1960, 1961, 1966, 1967, 1968, 1969,

248